WTF is Purpose?
And everything else I learned while trying to make
sense of it
By Sharoni Rosenberg Amszynowski
Foreword by Joan Antoni Melé

Editor in chief: Mauricio Electorat
Translation: Francisco Diaz Llases
Cover design: Giovanna Bacchiega / Belab
Interior design: Ebook Patagonia, Camila Salas and
Carolina Faget.
Text edition: María de los Ángeles Quinteros and
Trinidad Vicuña.

First Edition
ISBN 6-58325-39516-7 (paperback)

© Intelectual property registry No. 2021-A-3669

SHARONI ROSENBERG

PRAISE FOR WTF IS PURPOSE

"This book is a must-see and something that the purpose ecosystem was waiting for a long time, as it nourishes with knowledge and clarity a concept that until now had only been explained from the guts." **Nicolas Morales, Founder and CEO Trabajo con Sentido.**

"This book comes like rainwater in times of drought." **Joan Melé, Author and Founder of Ethical Banking in Latin America.**

"An essential and complete guide to the path to purpose, from someone who has made the journey with wonderful honesty and humility." **Josefa Monge, President Sistema B.**

"Spectacular book for anyone who wants to learn how to improve their life, to turn it into a work of art. It explains the why, the how and what to do to live with purpose."
Viktor Kuppers, Spanish author and speaker.

"The environmental, social and polarization crisis in which we live has led many of us to think about how we want to focus our energy. However, this search can be fraught with anxiety and platitudes. This amazing book offers a path to finding our purpose in a humane, compassionate and coherent way." **Felipe Chajin, Executive Director at Sistema B (B Corp Latinamerica).**

"Anyone who wants to undertake with purpose must start from their own personal process. This book is the perfect companion for that path." **Eduardo della Maggiora, Founder & CEO at Betterfly.**

"For those who are in the quest of their purpose, or those who have not yet considered it, or those who have already done their own exercise, this book will be a companion, a trigger or a retrospective view that will add methodology to the process. All those readers will see themselves humanly reflected and illuminated." **Daniel Vercelli, Co-Founder & Managing Partner at Manuia.**

"The author brings forward a question that sooner or later we will end up asking ourselves. And her book leads us to that personal answer, that will illuminate the rest of our lives." **Francisco Selamé, Partner PwC Chile.**

Purpose is always something to be shared, so I'm thankful, for your willingness to read my message. That alone makes me live my purpose.

If you want to share your concerns or opinions, or to delve on some of the subjects discussed in this book, you can contact me at my personal email address; I'll be more than happy to receive your queries at sharonirosenberg@gmail.com

CONTENT

Foreword by Joan Antoni Melé   11

Why Did I Write This Book?   15

Introduction   23

PART I:

WHAT IS PURPOSE   27

Chapter I: Questions That Remained Answerless   29

Chapter II: Happiness   37

Chapter III: Has Money Toppled *Eudaimonia?*   47

Chapter IV: Existential Vacuum   59

Chapter V: Starting A Path   67

PART II:

***TELOS*, A METHODOLOGY TO
DISCOVER YOUR OWN PATH TO PURPOSE**   75

Chapter VI: The Path To Purpose   77

Chapter VII: Who Am I?   105

    First Element: Authenticity   106

    Second Element: Passion   124

Chapter VIII: My Place In The World   143

    Third Element: Meaning Of Life   144

    Forth Element: Transcendence   163

Chapter IX: The *Telos* Core   185

PART III:
HOW THE PATH TO PURPOSE
IMPACTS YOUR LIFE   **189**
Chapter X: Motivation, The Best Sign That You're
On Your Way   191
Chapter XI: Spoiler Alert! Purpose Wasn't What I
Thought It Would Be, But I Discovered So Much More   203

APPENDIX   **219**
Appendix I: Ikigai And The Golden Circle   219
Appendix II: Definitions Of Purpose   224
Appendix III: Abraham Maslow's Theory Z   226
Appendix IV: Levels Of Transcendence   229

Table 1   234

Glossary   235

Acknowledgements   237
Rosh Hashanah Jewish Prayer   241

Quotes   242

FOREWORD BY JOAN ANTONI MELÉ

Every human being faces two great puzzles: the gateways of birth and death. We call them gateways because they signal a threshold between the sensorial world, a perceivable reality through the senses, and every other reality—the suprasensorial world. Before these two gateways, most human beings come up with multiple questions: will I somehow continue to exist after death? Will I be reunited with my loved ones who already passed away? Is there something before birth? In other words, is there a plan for this life?

Depending on how people answer these questions, life is lived one way or another. Life itself, whose length we ignore, becomes a puzzle. What is the meaning of life? Or, what purpose do I want to give it in the time that has been granted to me?

Throughout the history of mankind, and in very different ways in very different cultures, those questions have received varied approaches and tentative answers. In all ancient cultures, from the East, passing through what we now call Europe, to Abya Yala (name given to America by its native peoples), a knowledge of "another reality" has existed, what we sometimes call spiritual world, or suprasensible reality. But it wasn't a belief or a matter of faith; rather, human beings were able to perceive the existence of other beings with a different level of consciousness—and those they called gods. They would describe their experiences with that other reality using images, just like we narrate through images what we go through when we dream. Dreams are experiences from a non-sensitive reality, which can't be described in a sensitive way but rather need the use of images in order to be transmitted. That's how mythologies and legends were born. Even tales, which are for the current mentality only the fanciful inventions of our forefathers. But they're not. What happened was that we lost the capacity to interpret dream images.

The gradual loss of this ability to understand dream images, of imagination, progressively made way to the birth of thought as we understand it today. Seven or eight centuries before Christ, Greek philosophy arises, showing humans using one of their great abilities (thinking) to try and understand the world. But some hidden places remained, where the knowledge of that other reality, lost to most, was transmitted selectively only onto those students deemed worthy. And so we find the Eleusinian mysteries, the Samothracian mysteries, or the very temple of Apollo at Delphi, where the great maxim was inscribed: "Man, know thyself."

Aristotle's capacity for thought is astonishing. Some of his achievements, for instance in logic, have barely been surpassed to this day. During the Renaissance, that new capacity for thinking will take an even bigger leap, especially with the birth of modern science in the sixteenth century. If we hadn't lost our sense of wonder, we'd be constantly staring at scientific discoveries in awe, with our mouths open. How can the human being, just by thinking, discover universal laws that rule the earth and the cosmos, laws that already exist and have not been set by him? What is a law? Where do the laws that rule the universe come from?

Instead of answering these questions, science has focused on the "hows" over the "whys". This has meant an enormous development for science and technology, but it has also left that human without the answers to the two existential questions mentioned before. A materialistic and reductionist view has spread, and this has created our current society's way of life. According to that vision, this is just another step in the evolutionary process, with a few different genes compared to apes, and there's no more sense to life than a struggle for survival, which implies adapting to environmental conditions. And when death comes, this whole conglomerate of cells and genes that were once reunited by chance, will rot and nothing of what we once were will remain.

Of course, everyone is free to think whatever they want—but we must be aware that our ideas generate social models. If the idea that life is just a struggle for survival, that there's nothing after death, that a human being is just a set of genes grouped by chance, has really been instilled in me—then why should I care about other human beings or the environment? Why can't I just steal or kill? On what basis can I justify ethics? The only thing that I'll be interested in, if I share that opinion and I'm consistent with it, is myself and my own well-being. If not, let's ask ourselves why, in the 21st century, with all the technological and scientific knowledge at our disposal, and all the world's resources, we have more and more personal, social and environmental problems. Why is it that in the richest countries suicide has grown alarmingly? Why is it that people who have all the material resources come to such despair?

All our current conflicts and crises show us one thing: humanity, without losing what it has achieved through its great capacity for thought, urgently needs to broaden the horizon of its gaze and ask itself once again the original questions, which are so close to the essence of human beings.

In that sense, WTF is purpose?, by Sharoni Rosenberg, feels like rainwater in a drought. It comes at the right time, at kairós. Despite its author's age, it is a text of great maturity. I say this because it is not just another philosophical or self-help book, as they proliferate these days, but rather an eminently practical book both for an individual life and the development of organizations. The book serves directly as an approach to that "know thyself" and to find our place in the world.

I would dare say that this secret knowledge, which previously could only be found on some temples and hidden places, can be achieved today through a company. And not just by some people, but by any human being willing to lose their fear, to free themselves from prejudice and live authentically. Accordingly, this book is also a guide that can accompany directors, managers, and workers from those organizations that wish to become modern spaces for self-knowledge and social transformation. The solution to the world's problems will not arise merely from protests and electoral programs; it requires a radical change in human beings and current lifestyles.

Companies will only change the world once those who set them up become better people. This book can help turn them into agents of social transformation, as long as directors, managers and workers accept its propositions with honesty and courage. I welcome this book from my experience and commitment to ethics and the new economy, and I sincerely congratulate Sharoni Rosenberg for having had the initiative to write it.

Joan Antoni Melé.

WHY DID I WRITE THIS BOOK?

Before we get inside the universe of purpose, with all its facets and complexities, I would like to tell you why I wrote this book. A book that I hope will accompany all of those who wish to advance on their path to self-discovery and find their place in the world, in order to live a happier and more self-aware life.

I grew up hearing that making money and being recognized, overcoming others, was the key to success. And yet, these have never been the reasons why I get out of bed every morning. Don't get me wrong. I don't mean to say that I don't like to do a good job and grow professionally and earn a salary every month. I like all those things, and I don't intend to give them up.

However, if I check my personal history, I notice that those things have been a means and not an end. And that the moments that I have been the happiest have more to do with my relationship to other people than to material goods or personal achievements. I can honestly say that I have experienced greater happiness not when I have received something but when I have devoted myself to someone else and have somehow improved their lives or made them happier (even if it was for something minor, even if it was for just a moment).

But finding that out took me a long time.

When we are young, we seem to care more about what happens outside than inside ourselves. We are tormented by what others might say, about meeting parental expectations, feeling part of a group, recognized and accepted by others, etc. But as we become adults, many of us start experiencing things that make us look back and wonder, "How did I get here?" and "Where do I want to go?" This evolution and greater maturity lead us to questions that take us out of the inertia or automatic pilot that we were immersed in until that moment.

At thirty-one years old, I was what is usually known as a "successful" person. I had three beautiful daughters, a husband I love, a good job, and, in general, a good living situation. However, I felt a deep discomfort that wouldn't go away. Something made me feel incomplete, as if I were a divided subject. I felt like I wasn't doing everything that I could, and also that I wasn't doing everything that I wanted to do. What needed to change? How was I supposed to live? Why did I feel like that?

As Leo Tolstoy says in A Confession, these existential questions often come to those who apparently have a settled life. Or to those starting adulthood or facing their last years.

I was about to resign myself to keep leading this "happy" life. And then I found purpose.

A Phone Call

Five years ago, I was organizing my thirty-second birthday when the phone rang. It was Pablo, a friend of mine with whom I had worked ten years ago on social projects for the Fundación Techo, dedicated among other things to eradicating shanty towns.

We hadn't talked for a long time, so we caught up for a while until he got to what he wanted to discuss with me. He talked about purpose and how a new worldwide movement was forming that promoted companies that, in addition to making profits, were also good for the world. These are known as B Enterprises.

In that precise moment, a whole universe opened up before me. I still didn't fully understand what the word purpose meant, but it felt like I was at the start of a path where I would find many of the answers I was looking for.

After Pablo's phone call, a series of synchronies began. I would get legal advice requests for this type of company, and invitations to join the movement led by Sistema B[1]. I was also asked to take part of the team seeking to promote a bill recognizing this type of company—the "Sociedades de Beneficio e Interés Colectivo [Collective Benefit and Interest Companies] (BIC)" bill. And, among other things, I attended regional meetings in Lima, Puerto Varas and Mendoza. At the time I would say yes to any invitation of this sort. I wanted to explore, to learn, to share with different people, people I felt spoke my own language. Now I think the opportunities were always there. But it was only from that moment onwards that I became aware of what I wanted and that I learned to identify and seize those opportunities.

The Transformation

As I set out on this new path, I started feeling like I didn't care about the same things as I did before, or at least not in the same way. And while these changes were not evident to those around me, I felt them very deeply, and they made me think that something unprecedented was taking place. I wasn't that a new person was being born; on the contrary, it was as if **my real self** was appearing for the very first time.

The fundamental values that I already had were reaffirmed and several of my priorities shifted. Of course, I had always dreamed of contributing to a more just society, in which we would all care about the common good as much as our own well-being. But it was only then that I had the courage to make decisions that would allow me to effectively do something about it. Now I was willing to abandon my career as a tax attorney and venture into a less profitable or glamorous area, promoting this new way of doing business. I was always curious to do other things. Now I was courageous enough to make it happen.

These transformations also took place in my social life. People's intentions became more important than their actions, and that led me to value my environment in a different way. I wasn't looking as much at what people were doing; I cared more about why they did it. At the same time, it kept getting harder to remain indifferent towards people's cynicism or insincerity. I abandoned old friendships that felt superficial and inauthentic. I also started avoiding obligatory social gatherings and focused on those that I was really interested in. I gained greater empathy and stopped being the woman that would always be talking. Now I'd rather listen. I didn't find gossip about other people entertaining anymore. It was becoming more difficult for me to judge others, something that came quite easily before. I should also acknowledge that I was becoming a bit obsessed with purpose. Some friends said that I was now boring and that I showed no interest in any conversation unless it was about that.

The simplest things in life were now the ones I enjoyed the most: a good conversation with my grandmother, waking up in bed with one of my daughters, the warmth of the first days of Spring. I fell in love with nature, I planted my own garden, with vegetables and a compost system. If I was sad or discouraged, I no longer needed to go out and buy things; taking care of my plants was more than enough. Soon after, I started meditating. That was something that always felt a little too out there and never caught my attention. It was hard at first, and despite not quite understanding how it worked, I felt it was good for me and allowed me to connect with myself.

Being alone no longer made me feel anxious like it had before; in fact, I started enjoying it. I even dared to travel alone for the first time since I got married. I discovered the power of reading as a way of learning about the world. In fact, everything that I will share with you in this book has to do with that discovery. Reading became a way for me to be constantly educating myself.

Having lived abroad and belonging to the Jewish religion, the subject of diversity was dear to me. But now I saw it clearer than ever. It wasn't about tolerating or respecting others, it was about celebrating our differences as a central aspect in the richness of relationships. The more diverse my environment, the more I took advantage of that—and I found in the spiritual explanation of (non-religious) life the answer to that need for community with every human being.

As time went on, I started somehow benefiting from this conscious way of looking at life. I became more perceptive, creative, and my motivation increased every day. I had a great energy, I saw no limits to my dreams and ideals. And thus many new projects were born that I would've never dreamt of starting before.

Ever since then, it could be said that my decisions or the actions that I was taking were no longer guided by the need to satisfy my own interests. I began to see myself as an intermediary for something bigger, something hard to describe, and not necessarily graspable through strict reasoning. It was more of an act of faith. But don't get me wrong, an act of faith in the sense of accepting that there is something greater that is the cause of life which we can never really understand. Some refer to this as God, but throughout this book I will describe it as an Oceanic Feeling, the same way Romain Rolland defined it a century ago.

Perhaps the greatest gift of all were the new and profound friendships that flourished. I believed that at that point of life true friendships were no longer formed, but I was wrong. In the social world, or the world of purpose, connecting strangers that share interests is widely done. I started having "dates" with people that otherwise I would've never met. A meeting was enough for a bond to be created, which then led to projects or other kinds of synergy. It was as if we had known each other forever, for the mere fact that we shared a purpose.

Then, reading Abraham Maslow, I was again surprised to see that he describes this sequence of changes or transformations in his Theory Z (which we will discuss later). There are twenty-four of them, but I was most impressed by the one that deals with friendship. It says that people who seek to transcend in life "seem somehow to recognize each other, and to come to almost instant intimacy and mutual understanding even upon first meeting". I realized that Maslow describes each and every one of the things that happened to me, which confirmed that I wasn't so different, and that other people throughout the world and for a long time underwent similar processes.

The path to purpose is a starting point to reach a greater clarity about the choices we make throughout our lives, but above all to learn to choose that which really matters to us. It's a way of organizing our lives, of re-directing our expectations, our values or whatever we consider a success or a failure, and the things we need to be fully happy.

By the end of this journey, you are likely to experience a transformation that, among other things, will have changed your values and the way you narrate the story of your own life. This will happen in a conscious way, and you will learn that the path to purpose is a process and not a result… and that it can take months, years, your entire life.

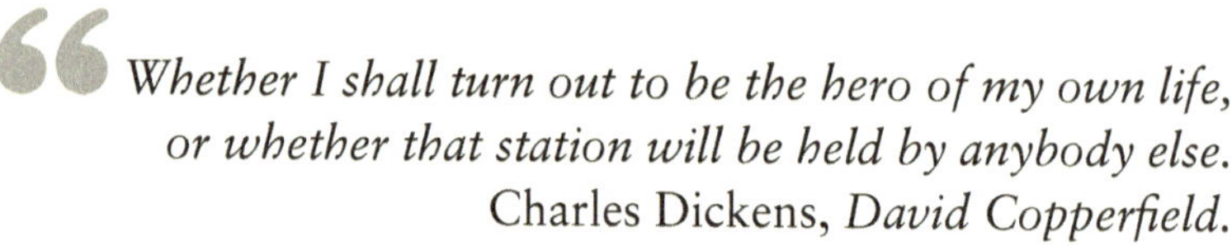

Whether I shall turn out to be the hero of my own life, or whether that station will be held by anybody else.
Charles Dickens, *David Copperfield.*

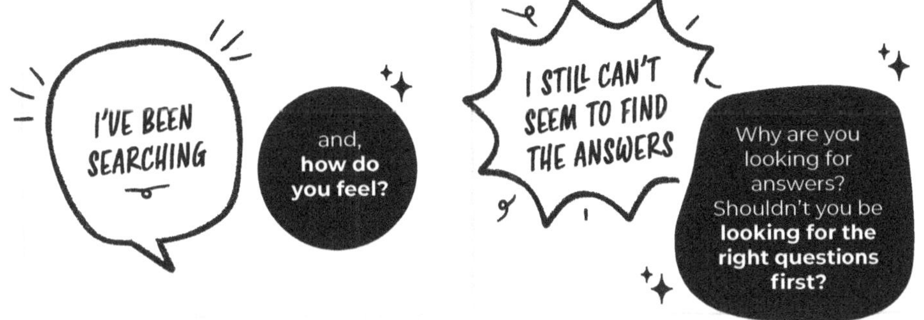
CONVERSATIONS BETWEEN MYSELF and MY CONSCIOUSNESS

CONSCIOUSNESS, TELL ME, SINCE YOU KNOW ME BETTER THAN ANYONE ELSE, "WHAT'S WRONG WITH ME?"

I need to know more before saying anything else. Keep searching

BUT HOW DO I SEARCH? HOW DO I KNOW WHAT'S HAPPENING TO ME AND WHERE THIS WILL LEAD ME?

Stop worrying so much about the future and start paying attention to your present. Start to listen to yourself

BUT HOW CAN I SPEND SO MUCH TIME ON SOMETHING THAT I DON'T EVEN KNOW WHAT IT IS? ARE YOU TELLING ME TO ISOLATE MYSELF FROM THE WORLD?

You will find the time. You will value every second spent on yourself. Stop being afraid of loneliness

AND HOW DO I EXPLAIN THIS TO MY FAMILY IF I DON'T EVEN UNDERTAND IT MYSELF?

They love you, and will understand if you need some space. And the time will come when they'll see in you what you're about to discover

A FEW MONTHS LATER:

I'VE BEEN SEARCHING

and, how do you feel?

I STILL CAN'T SEEM TO FIND THE ANSWERS

Why are you looking for answers? Shouldn't you be looking for the right questions first?

A YEAR LATER

CONSCIOUSNESS, I HAVE MANY QUESTIONS FOR YOU.

WHY DO I FEEL THIS VOID? IT'S AS IF SOMETHING WERE MISSING FOR ME TO BE COMPLETE. I BELIEVE A SPARK INSIDE OF ME, WHICH USED TO SHINE BRIGHTLY WHEN I WAS YOUNG, WENT OUT AND LEFT A VOID.

I HAVE A FEELING THAT WHAT I'M MISSING COULD BE MY PURPOSE, BUT I DON'T QUITE UNDERSTAND WHAT THAT MEANS. I HEARD THIS CONCEPT FROM PEOPLE I RESPECT AND ADMIRE, BUT WHENEVER I INQUIRE SOME MORE, IT'S AS IF NO ONE COULD EXPLAIN IT. AS IF IT WERE SOMETHING PEOPLE FEEL BUT CAN'T RATIONALIZE. I WANT TO KNOW WHAT IT IS. SOMETHING TELLS ME I'LL FIND MY ANSWERS THERE. A WAY OUT OF THIS VOID.

Then you're on the right track. You have a direction to follow.

BUT I'M AFRAID. VERY AFRAID.

The fear of suffering is worse than the suffering itself. You're afraid because you care, and that's human. But fear can't stop you. Go. Keep going. Take a chance. That alone will mean you're living your path to Purpose.

What are you afraid of?

I'M AFRAID I'LL LOSE WHAT I ALREADY HAVE. I'M AFRAID I WON'T FIND WHAT I'M LOOKING FOR. EVEN WORSE: I'M AFRAID I'LL FIND OUT THERE'S NOTHING ELSE.

INTRODUCTION

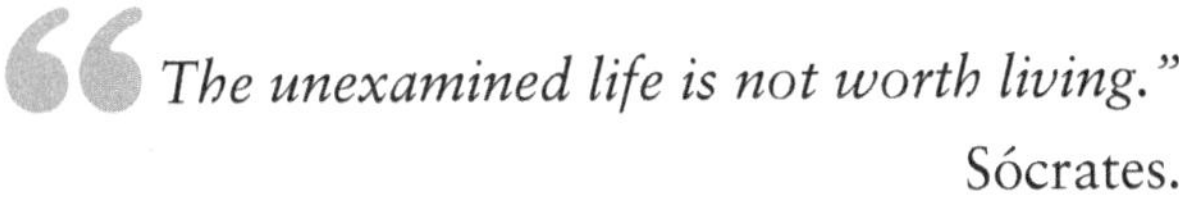

> *The unexamined life is not worth living."*
>
> Sócrates.

Human beings are a complex species (which is not the same as being complicated). Life is made up of diverse elements which must relate to each other so that we can live in harmony. And yet we are often satisfied with simple answers to questions that would require further analysis. On top of this, we get used quite easily to the comfort behind simplicity, to things being handed out to us. That's the case with the subject at hand. To know and discover our relationship to purpose requires a lot of reflection and self-knowledge, since to fully understand it would necessarily imply to scrutinize our human complexity. It's a process that starts at the most intimate and personal level and then opens up to the world, unfolding all of its splendor.

What the Hell Is Purpose?

As I was trying to come up with a title for this book, many times I thought it should be that one: *What the Hell Is Purpose?* It was probably not the most subtle one, specially not for a more conservative Latin American readers (The name is Spanish is *Purpose Was Not what I Expected: but it gave me more than I bargained for*). However, in this English version I felt more free to name it WTF is Purpose?, because that is really how I felt about it.

Although purpose is a concept widely used by people, businesses and institutions, I was intrigued by the variety of meanings given to it. In fact, there's so many meanings as there are sources to consult, and all of them share a rather expository nature. They don't conceptualize the subject and they present somewhat partial points of view.

Let's start with the first thing you do when you don't know something: Google. There we'll find a series of concepts, such as:

- Purpose of a human being is whatever meaning he ascribes to his life.
- Purpose answers existential questions such as "why" and "what for."
- Purpose is to move towards a goal or project that we wish to achieve.

These definitions didn't explain what was happening to me. They weren't enough. It was all I was able to find, but I needed to know so much more. While purpose might sound like a relatively simple concept, I felt that it was hard to explain holistically.

I must admit that our ability as human beings to talk about things we don't understand is surprising. I talked about purpose with everyone, but now I see how far I was from really understanding what I was talking about. While I was writing this book, I reached out to several "experts" on the subject and asked them what it meant for them or how they defined it. Only one of them was able to outline a concept beyond a brief definition. I can't even tell you what happened when I asked them how they would define a company with purpose. I didn't get a single coherent or clear answer. Although that's a subject for another book, I hope.

Several authors have speculated with a definition. Most agree that purpose is important because:

1/ It gives us direction.
2/ It allows us to find meaning in our lives.

3/ It invites us to transcend by contributing to something bigger than ourselves.

This information was a good starting point, but it still felt insufficient. What does each of these statements mean?

I also came across authors, articles and blogs on the internet that brought purpose closer to other concepts such as passion, vocation, a spark, a life calling. I wondered if these ideas were different from each other or simply different ways of referring to the same thing. Precisely, the writing of this book has made me realize to what extent purpose is a concept that surpasses, in richness and complexity, all the previous ideas.

On the other hand, I found people in the process who were discouraging. For many, these are issues that belong to the first world and which don't apply to developing countries such as Latin Americans. But it only takes one look around to realize that we have fallen victims to our own egos, creating a false self-image in order to feel protected against the world's aggressions. We have also fallen victims to success' voracity. The numbers for mental health problems associated with stress, anxiety disorders, and depression, have gone through the roof in the last thirty years, despite an increasing GDP per capita. While we can't deny that material deficiencies still exist, we are also witnessing another kind of crisis, an existential and spiritual one.

I understand the initial resistance, but I have the certainty that our great barrier, if we are to keep advancing along this path, is to really find out what we mean when we talk about purpose. After a lot of searching I realized that the only way to grow and fully understand the concept was to delve in different disciplines or sciences. The answers weren't fully within positive psychology, sociology, anthropology, philosophy, theology or neuroscience, but rather, partially, in all of them.

A great challenge began right there. I had to study not only what was available to the general public but also all of the specialized literature I could find—dissertations, scientific articles, books on philosophy, among others. Then I had to learn to unlearn and forget everything I had ever read and heard about it, and start studying all of this seriously. I was guided by a single goal: to get a holistic vision of what purpose is, so that I could culminate the transformation I was going through. That way, I would find out what my own purpose in life was, if there was any. In this book, I want to share my results with you.

> *All knowledge pursued merely for the enrichment of personal learning and the accumulation of personal treasure leads you away from the path; but all knowledge pursued for growth to ripeness within the process of human ennoblement and cosmic development brings you a step forward."*
>
> Rudolf Steiner.

PART I:
WHAT IS PURPOSE

Questions That Remained Answerless

> *The mind is like a parachute:
> it only works when it's open."*
> Albert Einstein.

When I started my investigation, everyone was talking about the Japanese concept of *ikigai* and Simon Sinek's *Golden Circle* (you can read more about them in Appendix I). I read and studied them too, seeking for the answers to the many questions I had. However, although they were both inspiring and served as a gateway into the matter, I still couldn't tie up all the loose ends. Sinek examines the importance behind the "why" in the things we do, and connects it to the emotional part of our brain. Ikigai refers to that which we love, what we are good at, our contribution to the world and what we can get paid for.

But I had the feeling that purpose should also contain important concepts like intention, self-awareness, our identity, virtue or moral behavior, our values and motivations. Nor could I understand whether purpose and the meaning of life were the same thing or not. Simultaneously, I had doubts about how purpose related to love and our concept of what success and happiness are. The other thing that I didn't quite get was what they meant when they discussed transcendence—it wasn't enough for me to know that it was something bigger than ourselves. Surely there was much more to dig into, something somehow related to spirituality (another concept I was having trouble processing).

After thinking about it a lot, and after sorting out all the doubts that were piling up in my head, I reached the conclusion that I had to tackle purpose by answering two big questions:

- What is purpose?
- How do I find my purpose?

The first question will be developed throughout this chapter, whereas the second will be answered later.

The Meaning of the Word

First, let's see what the dictionary says, a habit of mine from my days as a lawyer. According to the Oxford Advance Dictionary, purpose (from the Old French *porpos*, indicating aim or intention, and *proposer*, to put forth) can be defined as:

1/ an intention.
2/ an objective, a reason for doing something.

This is of the outmost importance: purpose can be an intention and an objective. And while these definitions are rather concise (as definitions usually are) they provide us with a good starting point. On the one hand, we have our will directed towards an end. And we also have the objective, which an action is directed at. This may sound very abstract and philosophical, but there truly is "something" inside us all wishing to be expressed in the outer world. And it seems that when there is a consistency between what we genuinely are and what we do in our daily lives, we feel as if we were living our purpose. Later on, we will see that these two things are not mutually exclusive, and that intention and objective represent the two sides of a single concept.

This intention directed at an objective is something Aristotle already noticed. The Greek philosopher believed that everything in life is oriented towards an ultimate goal, and he used the concept of teleology (from the Greek *telos*, meaning purpose) to refer to the doctrine which studies purpose of things instead of their causes. Aristotle was absolutely convinced that, in order to understand a thing, we must understand it in relation to its ultimate goal. To him, every living being in this planet, be it a person, animal or plant, has a goal to strive for and, therefore, a path towards which to perfect themselves.

This was already a significant progress in terms of my research. I knew for sure that all things that exist have a purpose, something they aspire to become. For instance, Aristotle said that purpose of an acorn is to become an oak; and that of a caterpillar, to become a butterfly. In other words, he suggests that purpose of each species is the same—the reason why they exist or came to the world.

But, if all species have their own purpose, what would that of human beings be? My research was facing a turning point. Soon I'll tell you why. First, let's go back a little.

What I Thought Was True

Before I asked that question, and based on the information at hand, I was of the opposite opinion. I had made up my mind that each human being had their own purpose in life. A single unique guiding principle for each single unique person. After having carried out dozen of online surveys, which usually promise things like "find your purpose in five steps" or "solve your existential queries in less than thirty minutes," everything pointed at purpose being a unique phrase that would forever define my life.

Finding that phrase was the only thing I could think of at the time. They all said it should be as brief as a twitter tweet (hopefully no more than forty characters) and contain that which I was called to do in this world. I had to formulate a sentence such as:

- Make the world a better place for mankind.
- Save the world through education.
- Be compassionate with yourself and the rest of the universe.
- End poverty in Africa.

These blogs promised that if I was able to draw up such a phrase, my happiness would take off like a rocket and nothing and no one could ruin that for me. I would never again for any reason feel the emptiness that was consuming me from the inside. It was an invitation to reach nirvana.

I can say this now with some distance and a sense of humor. But a few years ago, any simplistic explanation and solution to what was for me a crucial subject would make me feel helpless and frustrated. For a long time I was trapped searching for the "perfect phrase." As much as I wanted to find it, I never did.

At one point I came to the realization that the pressure and anxiety I was feeling by trying to summarize my purpose, that which would define the rest of my life, in a single sentence, was too much to bear. The anguish of not knowing who I was became so strong that I felt ashamed of sharing it with others: I was afraid it wouldn't quite reflect my identity or, worse, if I ever changed it, it would make me seem insecure. I think the obsession became even more severe in others: there was always someone who didn't want to share their phrase with the rest of the group, perhaps fearing they would reveal more than necessary about themselves, or that their phrase could be stolen by some opportunist, and thus stealing with it a part of their identity.

Despite my confusion and insecurity, I managed to phrase my first sentence of purpose. Picking up on how happy I had been working on social projects, and also based on the examples seen on multiple superficial blogs, my sentence read: Helping vulnerable people in order to reduce poverty in the country. At first it was very gratifying. I thought I had finally reached the goal. For a second, I felt like a captive fish that had been returned to its river. After a few weeks, though, the sentence I'd written, which had made me feel so free, wasn't as convincing.

I tried not taking it to heart. After all, who gets it right the first time? Although a part of me felt identified with purpose I had originally stated, I couldn't stop thinking about one thing: where did my family fit in all of this? purpose is supposed to be just one, and for life. So how could I leave out the most important part of my life?

At that time, reflection and meditation led me to conclude that the phrase should be oriented to what I enjoyed doing the most: connecting with others and giving them my all. It didn't make a difference if it was my daughter, a girl I had just met at an orphanage or an intern at the office. Whatever the context, aside from the obvious differences between certain affective bonds, I felt that my purpose was "to give love to all people unconditionally."

I was at peace with this statement. What made me feel at ease was that it included the two most important aspects of my life: my family and a job in which I could contribute something. But once again, a few months later, the same thing happened: something didn't feel right. At the time, I was dedicated to helping several foundations with their legal issues and every so often I didn't even get to meet the people behind each project. I was very happy just knowing I had made their lives simpler and that my knowledge was serving something I deemed important.

By then, I felt as if I had failed. This led me back to my captivity. I would wonder: "What if I never find my purpose?" I knew I had to adapt my sentence again and I was very confused by that. Only one thing was clear: things didn't work the way blogs presented them. Something deep inside of me was telling me that purpose couldn't be just one for life, unique and unchanging. It seemed to me that life was just too complex and purpose couldn't be reduced to a single perfect line.

I kept trying for a while. I felt that many sentences could reflect my essence and what I had come into this world for. On the one hand, verbs like contribute, help, inspire and improve; on the other, words as common as love, creating, making others happy, felt appropriate. Other more sophisticated concepts, like consciousness, spirituality and transcendence also made sense. They were all calling out to me for my sentence of purpose. At the same time, asking closer friends, we all seemed to have very similar statements. Something similar to what happens to companies when they state they mission or vision: it's hard to distinguish one from the next, they're all extremely similar on paper. Words weren't the important thing. There had to be something else.

This whole thing seemed like a dead end. I was going in circles without getting anywhere. Firmly, I started questioning if finding purpose was about getting to that unique sentence, or if it was deeper than that. For a long time, I had been looking for my purpose basing the search on what I did, my projects, my job, and an inner voice kept telling me that purpose wasn't something to be sought outside, in the outer world, in an activity, but rather something personal and intimate, like a calling to self-knowledge, to finding my real identity. Only then could I really live my purpose.

I was starting to lose hope when I bumped again into a sentence by Aristotle which I had read many times, but that only then made real sense to me:

"Purpose of human beings is happiness".

Going back to the beginning, it was at that moment that I was able to finally answer the question about purpose of human beings.

Just like Aristotle had signaled purpose of acorns and caterpillars, he had done the same things regarding the human species. If what he had said was true, I thought, then searching for the perfect sentence would make no sense. purpose couldn't be about seeking each person's own, since we'd all share the same one, happiness. Or, as he called it, *Eudaimonia*.

Happiness

After doing some thinking, I could see the logic behind this premise and I found several other philosophers, psychologist or spiritual referents, like the Dalai Lama, who agreed

For those of us who are parents, this shouldn't come as a surprise. Not surprisingly, during our deepest conversations we find ourselves telling our children that their happiness is the most important thing for us. Our parents said the same thing. After all, who doesn't want to be happy?

Everything I was unearthing made a lot of sense to me. We all want to be happy, there's no doubt about it. The problem is that, for some reason, we have stopped taking that idea seriously. Despite how important it is for our lives, we often refer to our own happiness almost mechanically, as if we were greeting someone with the question "how are you?", out of habit, not really wanting to know the answer. We use the word happiness but we never take the time to think about its meaning, its importance for our well-being, and how we can reach it.

You could say that, at that point in my personal search, two things were clear to me, and they would help me answer the first of the two questions that I raised at the beginning:

1/ All human beings share a purpose.

2/ That purpose is happiness.

This leads us to a fundamental question:

What is happiness?

Happiness

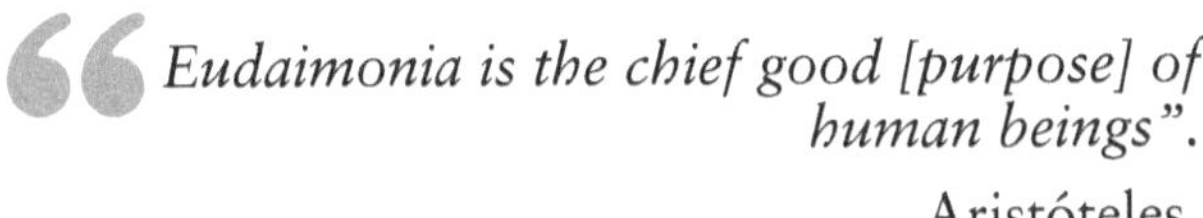

*Eudaimonia is the chief good [purpose] of
human beings".*

Aristóteles.

There are hundreds of thousands of books dealing with
happiness. It's a theme that has always obsessed philosophers,
essayists, playwrights and poets. Interestingly enough, most
of the books that allude to it go back to its origin, as far as
Ancient Greece. Back then, people believed there were two
types of happiness[2]: hedonism and *Eudaimonia*.

Hedonism is a Greek word, which contains the prefix
hedone (meaning pleasure) and the suffix ismoque (doctrine).
As stated by its name, it's a philosophical doctrine that places
pleasure as the supreme good of human life. A hedonist is
always looking to get closer to pleasure and farther away from
pain.

While for the most part it was the Greeks who developed
the concept, the doctrine predates them. It goes as far back
as the 11th century BCE in India, where the Charvaka school
of philosophy postulated that happiness existed to the extent
that sensory pleasures could be experienced for the longest
amount of time. For example, they discussed the enjoyment
caused by a delicious meal, the company of young girls, fine
clothing or exquisite perfumes. For them, if something involved
deprivation or penance, it didn't contribute to this sort of life[3].

For that same reason, Aristotle considered that a hedonic life, based merely on individual pleasure, was a vulgar and primitive thing.

> In hedonism, happiness is synonymous with pleasure.

This lifestyle often seems attractive to most, at least at first. On a closer inspection, like Aristotle says, more than a happy life, it's an easy one. Besides, while it can be an end in itself, it's not stable in time, nor is it unique to man (any animal can feel pleasure) and many times it doesn't depend on oneself—all characteristics that he says are fundamental to the human purpose. That's why he discarded it as a philosophical option for happiness, choosing *Eudaimonia* instead.

Eudaimonia

Well-being, blossoming or fulfillment

This word, hard to spell, pronounce and understand, etymologically contains the words eu (good) and daimon (spirit), and refers to well-being, which includes both happiness, seen as sensory pleasure, and fullness, understood in its spiritual dimension.

The term prevails through Classical Antiquity but dissipates during the Middle Ages (when catholic dogma prevails). It reappears when the medieval catholic system of thought shatters (somewhere around the 12 and 13th centuries) with the emergence of the first humanist philosophers, who place the human being at the center of life. The latter does not imply denying the existence of God, but rather presupposes a non-dogmatic relationship to faith. From there on, the idea of happiness becomes part of the philosophical repertoire of Enlightened thought: Jean-Jacques Rousseau, Diderot, Kant, Condorcet—they all believe in the perfectibility of the person, that is to say, that humanity, progressively and through the use of reason, can move towards its own perfection: *Eudaimonia*.

It consists of a life well-lived, both for oneself and for those around us. It's the kind of happiness which is uniquely human, an invitation not only to live a pleasant life from a sensory standpoint, but also to include well-being in its most spiritual dimension. It is a kind of happiness which gives meaning to our lives[4], and where it is not enough to seek for our own well-being; it goes beyond that.

If hedonistic happiness comes down to feeling good, *Eudaimonia* can be defined as being and doing good.

Eudaimonia occurs in the making, in the human experience in relation to us and to others. It lives in our virtuous actions and not in the world of ideas, as Plato stated. We are happy when we are just, solidary, generous, tolerant, promote equality, beauty and, above all, love and kindness.

Therefore, it is not enough to know what the ultimate goal of human beings is; what matters are the actions taken in order to get there. Not just any action: the virtuous ones that lead us to act properly.

Aristotle thinks that a virtuous life is not limited to important characters who are either in positions of power or have achieved great deeds. According to his conception, any form of service to others is potentially a virtuous activity.

For this Greek philosopher, *Eudaimonia* is an end in itself: life's supreme good. That which people choose before anything else, unlike richness, professional success or power, for instance, which are desired to reach that goal but not as goals in themselves. This kind of happiness, when present, makes us feel complete. In other words, as if we were living the way we're supposed to live. Somehow we feel a profound certainty and know we're doing the right thing and walking a path that is properly ours.

Unlike mere pleasure, happiness derived from *Eudaimonia* has a lasting effect, since it is a state maintained over time. Reaching it requires a process of reflection, during which we integrate events that occur at different times, but which give meaning to our lives, even if they take effort or pain[5]. For instance, a student that is doing his PhD abroad, in a foreign language, having to make an extra effort to be at the expected level, decides to take this more difficult path precisely because of the satisfaction that such a challenging experience provides to himself.

Perhaps what distinguishes *Eudaimonia* from all the other ways of conceiving happiness, is that it transcends the individual itself. It presupposes a need to love and surrender oneself that goes beyond the physical or what can be understood through reasoning.

For that very same reason, Aristotle considered *Eudaimonia* the authentic form of happiness, the most noble and honorable of them all.

> *Eudaimonia* is the happiness of the soul.

Unfortunately, the concept disappears in the 20th century, and happiness becomes limited to the sphere of the individual, in the sense of a harmonic relationship between the subject and the world, based on satisfying needs and in pleasure.

In our consumerist society, the majority prioritizes satisfying their needs and personal desires through the path of least resistance, and they make other people's well-being irrelevant to their goal.

A conceptual extremism might be the biggest problem with this lifestyle, since it equivocally relates pleasure and pain: it assimilates effort with pain and idleness with pleasure[6], as if there were no satisfaction to be found in effort or boredom in idleness.

This turns the consumerist into a slave, someone who has an ideal of happiness that will eventually get truncated, since this way of life does not lead to real happiness. A lifestyle with these characteristics poses a problem, or at least a challenge for current society, since it doesn't provide individuals with a better well-being nor does it contribute to building a better society.

What Does Science Say?

Although *Eudaimonia* seemed consistent with the kind of happiness I was searching, it was important for me to understand what the recent science was saying, so that I could get a more complete picture of what I was learning and could also confirm what the Greeks pointed out. Let us see what the different sciences have to say in this regard.

Humanistic Psychology

Abraham Maslow (1908, Brooklyn), the humanistic psychologist, developed the concept of happiness on the basis of human needs. Hierarchy, represented in the shape of a pyramid, places human needs from the most pressing to the highest. He builds it based on the premise that every subject able to grow freely and in harmony (considering the political and social context of their environment) will naturally seek to satisfy their needs.

Each need is represented by a level of the pyramid. Progression can be achieved as we develop physic, psychologic and spiritually[7]. Physiological needs (also called basic needs) predominate in infancy and early childhood. Safety, belonging and self-esteem, called intermediate, prevail in late childhood and early adulthood. And those of self-realization and transcendence, called highest or spiritual, appear in adulthood[8].

Maslow's pyramid
Human needs

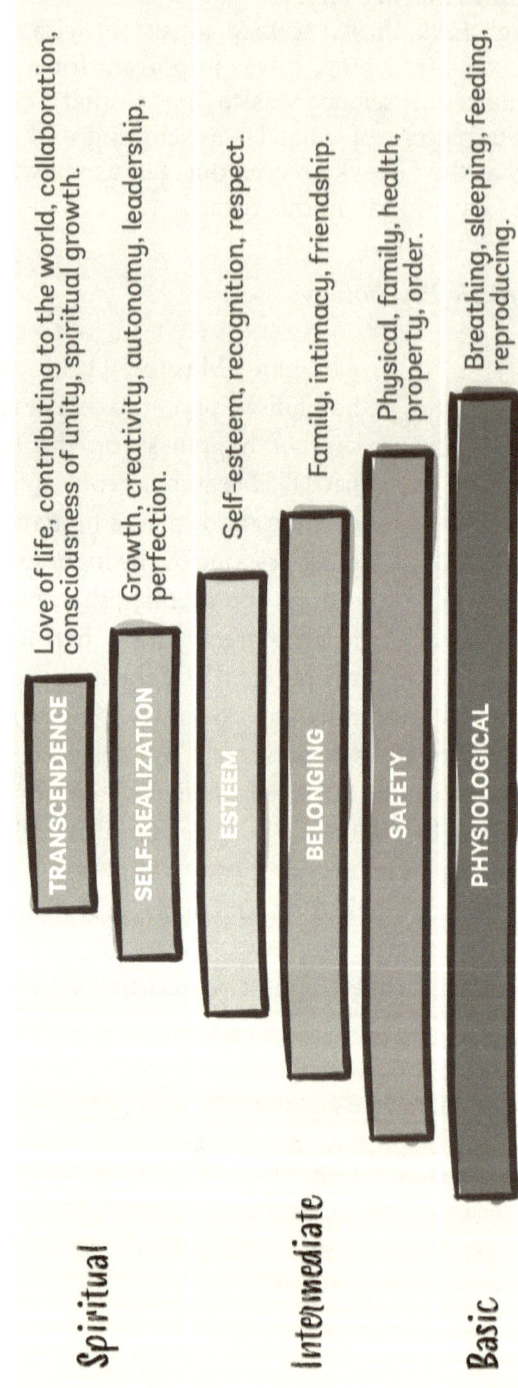

Maslow knew that human beings seek to preserve their own lives, and so he placed the need for survival at the most basic level[9]. But he also knew that we seek a constant physical, emotional and spiritual growth. Therein lies the importance of developing ourselves in every aspect of life, so that we can reach what he deems as true happiness.

During much of his professional career, Maslow claimed that the highest human need was that of self-realization, which he understood as the need for people to perfect their abilities to the maximum, increasing the use of their skills, strength and potential in general. However, in the latter stage of his career he added an even higher level: transcendence.

He adds that soon after satisfying the physiological, safety, belonging and esteem needs, a new dissatisfaction and unrest develops. And it can only be overcome by doing what we are potentially capable of doing and putting it at the service of others. As he describes it, if they want to be at peace with themselves, a musician must make music, an artist must paint, and a poet must write. A human being must be what they can be[10], and then make what they do available to others.

Maslow's works are scattered through different sources, which is why most of his material doesn't show his findings on transcendence. Most of the available images of the pyramid stop at self-realization and ignore that whole other level.

Positive Psychology[11]

Positive psychology is a science that was formally recognized as such two decades ago. It aims to understand and describe how happiness and general well-being can be cultivated. It is different from cognitive psychology in that it doesn't focus solely on diseases. In recent times, the theme of happiness has been more developed by this area of science. And while it doesn't use the word *Eudaimonia*, it certainly takes the baton when it comes to its principles. It talks of well-being, flourishing, fullness, authentic or happiness.

Important figures such as Martin Seligman, Carol Ryff, Mihaly Csikszentmihalyi and Tal Ben-Shahar, among others, have researched and created valuable content related to subjective well-being, understood as the evaluation a person makes of their own lives. That is to say, tending to determine how happy one think one is[12].

Martin Seligman, psychologist, co-founder of positive psychology, and promoter of the PERMA theory of Well-being[13], argues that the vast majority of people, as long as they're free and without suffering, yearn for happiness. For him, happiness is a complex phenomenon which is made up by maximizing positive emotions (the hedonist dimension of happiness) but also by the appearance of other elements akin to *Eudaimonia*, like engagement with what we're doing, good relationships, self-realization and feeling part of something bigger than ourselves.

Along these lines, university professor Tal Ben-Shahar, one of the leading experts on happiness and teacher to one of the most popular courses in Harvard, is deeply convinced that a life of flourishing can be achieved by living in a way that we contribute both to our own well-being and that of others[14]. Ben-Shahar believes basic, intermediate and spiritual needs to be equally important. A person without a livelihood and someone living in solitude or selfishly have no chance of being happy.

He bases his theory of happiness on two sources: Sigmund Freud's pleasure principle, and Viktor Frankl's principle that the meaning of life is the main cause behind human motivation and well-being. The sum of the two corresponds to true *Eudaimonia*. On the other hand, he also claims that a life in the pursuit of transcendence intensifies our sense of pleasure in everything we do.

Neuroscience

Eudaimonia finds its most rational explanation in the functioning of our own brain. Different studies in neuroscience have shown that the human body can release, basically, four types of hormones that contribute to the feeling of happiness: those which promote our individual well-being, namely endorphin and dopamine; and those which promote a collective well-being, serotonin and oxytocin.

1. Hormones which promote individual well-being They contribute to our survival, for example in helping us get shelter and food, and taking us where we need to go. They are present in every animal.	**2. Hormones which promote collective well-being.** They reveal our nature as social beings and see that we make progress as a species. They explain our desires of wanting to belong, feeling loved and transcend. They are only found in human beings.
1.1. Endorphin: counteracts pain by increasing our physical capacity to resist it. It is obtained, for example, by exercising or laughing.	**2.1 Serotonin:** originates self-esteem, the ability to feel loved and capable of doing great things. Reinforces intimacy bonds, making us feel responsible for them. Makes us value and promote our environment. Can be increased by maintaining a balanced and healthy life, good nutrition and doing meditation exercises.
1.2 Dopamine: guides us towards fulfilling our goals and wishing to be better. The bigger the effort, the greater the release of hormones will be when the goal is achieved. It is highly addictive and is obtained, for instance, by eating.	**2.2 Oxytocin:** they call it the "love hormone" as it encourages us to be generous and empathetic. It makes us feel good every time we're supportive and grateful, and also when others act that way towards us. It inspires us to be collaborative, trusting, good people. It also fosters a virtuous chain, since the more we do things for others, the more we want to keep doing them. It is promoted through physical contact, like breastfeeding or hugging[15].

These hormones are so powerful that every time we feel joy, it is highly likely due to one or more of them circulating through our veins. In terms of duration, they vary: the individual ones make you feel a short and intense discharge, while the collective last longer and provide a more stable and permanent feeling of well-being, something typical of *Eudaimonia*.

Now that we have delved into the meaning of happiness, the question that we should ask ourselves is this: Have we been searching for pleasure or *Eudaimonia*?

Has Money Toppled *Eudaimonia?*

> *I think everybody should get rich and famous and do everything they ever dreamed of so they can see that it's not the answer".*
>
> Jim Carrey.

Now that we have covered the philosophical and scientific background of happiness, we must analyze our relationship to it in the past few decades. Sometimes I feel as if we were tennis balls hitting a court wall, over and over again, with a flawless technique but unable to get to the other side of the court. We train and refine our skills, but that's it, we don't chance playing the game.

What happens in our consumerist society is that there's an ever-growing imbalance between what is believed to be happiness and what really is. We think that having more will make us happy and we find ourselves caught focusing on ourselves, on wanting more, owning more, accumulating more, distancing ourselves from what we truly need.

This scenario forces us to review our relationship with money and understand that, while it can help us reach happiness, it can also take it away from us.

Undoubtedly, there is an important relationship between money and well-being. After all, we have been using it to exchange goods and services for over ten thousand years[16]. This convention was born to replace the old barter system and gives way to the subsequent financial circuits and transactions between strangers, among other benefits. In that sense, money has enhanced human interactions, satisfied needs and increased our well-being significantly, thus leading us to be happier.

But his premise, which may sound obvious and even redundant, has lost its essence in recent centuries. Money has become an end in itself rather than a means. The guiding principle seems to be "the more money I accumulate, the more I can consume; and the more I consume, the greater my well-being should be." That's as absurd as thinking that we live in order to breathe, feed ourselves or sleep.

The following questions originate from this:

- When did we start considering money the unit for measuring our well-being?
- How has this affected our happiness?

Let's see some explanations that can shed light over these questions:

The Desire to Accumulate

Looking back at the evolution of the human being, back when we were hunters and gatherers, accumulating food was crucial to our survival[17]. Weathering winter depended on the amount of food gathered throughout the year. So, accumulating became part of the survival strategy.

We have held to this habit to this day. However, although we continue to accumulate, we no longer do so as a means to ensure our survival. Money has become the means to ensure our survival, but instead of accumulating in order to live, we have acquired the habit of living in order to accumulate.

According to a study conducted by Easterlin and Sawangfa[18], money increases people's well-being until their basic needs are covered. Once these are met, however, our well-being doesn't increase as our income does. An increase in the income of those who earn between six and seventeen thousand dollars a year, implies a correlative increase in their well-being. But once the threshold of seventeen thousand dollars is topped, said correlation starts to decline. After that, earning more money becomes less and less important to our feeling of well-being[19].

Our Erratic Ability to Simulate Experiences

In his TED talk, "The Surprising Science of Happiness", Dan Gilbert, a psychologist from Harvard University, explains that our beliefs about things that make us happy are usually mistaken[20]. He says that the prefrontal cortex of our brain has, among other functions, the capacity to create an "experience simulator" that allows us to imagine or visualize things before they take place in real life. It is a faculty that can be very useful at times, as it inhibits us from potentially harmful situations (like diving into a river in the middle of winter), but which can also lead us to make mistakes.

To prove his point, Gilbert invited his audience to do an exercise. He showed them two different scenarios on a big screen. The first had someone winning the lottery, while in the other someone became paraplegic after a car accident. The audience had to compare both individuals and quickly choose who they thought was the happiest. The only information they had was that, before this event had taken place, they both had the same level of happiness, comparatively speaking.

At first glance, the audience would predictably choose the winner of the lottery as the happiest of the two, and in fact they did. But when Gilbert proceeded to show their lives a year after the event, the audience's perception changed radically: they both enjoyed exactly the same level of well-being as they did before winning the lottery or having had the accident, respectively.

The explanation for this, says Gilbert, is that the moments of pleasure or hedonism (like winning the lottery or buying a new house) increase our well-being for a very short span of time.

According to his research, the feeling of joy from a pleasant event lasts for as long as one month. Which would explain how, after a year, the individuals from the exercise were back to the same level of well-being they had before the events[21]. If the winner of the lottery was an unhappy person before winning it, chances are that he will remain being one. Gilbert concludes that the relative weight of these high-pleasure-discharge events is not big enough to alter our reality, despite our "experience simulator" wanting us to believe otherwise.

This happens all the time. We have that old saying, "the grass is always greener on the other side," for a reason. It is also a problem for those on the other side of the coin, namely those being judged by their financial situation. I know the case of Alan, a twenty-eight-year-old who inherited a fortune from his grandfather. The amount of money is considerable; in practice, he wouldn't need to work another day and would still be able to maintain his level of expenditure. To the eyes of the world, his situation is enviable. Although it is true that he is "set for life", he still wants to be productive, like his friends are; however, no one from his circle takes him seriously, since they can't understand that he wants to work when he doesn't need to.

Those who meet Alan assume that he lives a happy life. However, he disagrees. He just wants to have a normal life, a reason to get up every morning, to feel proud of his own achievements. He feels a deep void and, since no one takes him seriously, has come to doubt his own abilities. He dares not try anything new and feels frustrated. He tells me that at times he wishes he could go on living the life he had before, and that no one would notice the inheritance he received. Despite what people might think, in Alan's case money has created a bigger void than anything else.

Communicational Candor

The same greed for money and for being able to consume more and more, has been fed by the information we get in the media and on social networks. We believe everything we are told, for example when we are shown a conditioner that will make our hair look like that of our favorite actress, or the energetic drink that will turn us into better soccer players, or the perfect vacation that will solve all our family conflicts. We are willing to pay for basically any product that promises to get us closer to our longed-for happiness... and those who work in marketing know this.

We have let advertising dictate our guidelines, even when we know these infomercials don't intend to educate or advise us but rather sell us something, anything. The same thing happens with social networks: their objective is not to show us how our friends and close ones really live, but rather small, embellished bits from every-day life, in which everyone wants to look like they're doing great all the time, even if they aren't. The more we lack something, the more we try to prove we don't. We know that to be true because we fall into the same behavior. Despite that, even knowing that it's all a sham, our insecurity feeds an overwhelming level of stress and frustration.

Money Collaterals

What many haven't yet internalized is that consumerism and materialism can act to our detriment. Their effect on us is not insignificant. A series of studies has shown that material aspirations can even lower our life satisfaction levels[22]. Research done by Seligman and Diener during 2004 in the US show that materialistic people tend to downplay their interpersonal relationships and are constantly unhappy with their income[23].

A similar study investigated different lottery winners and showed that people with unlimited purchasing power were less able to enjoy the simpler things in life[24]. Little by little, they had lost their sense of wonder. On top of that, they tended to take each of their privileges for granted, which in turn made them lose the sense of fulfillment that comes from being grateful.

Another research conducted by American psychologist Tim Kasser showed that people with aspirational values (relative to money, social status and power) carry a higher risk of depression and are more prone to mental disorders[25]. Kasser claims that materialism produces lower levels of well-being, since it can be associated with low levels of self-esteem, empathy and intrinsic motivation, as well as high levels of narcissism and social comparison, which brings about greater conflicts in interpersonal relationships[26].

As seen, studies along this line of research are abundant, and yet the popular belief that money makes us happy remains deeply ingrained in our culture. Proof of this is that, despite each generation being richer than the last, well-being indices are only getting worse[27].

Renowned Chilean psychiatrist Ricardo Capponi calls this human phenomenon of always wanting more, even when it doesn't make us happier, "hedonistic adaptation." Capponi points out that our sensory organs, which let us feel pleasure, are made in such a way that a repeated stimulus loses strength over time. It's as if the organ got tired and stopped being stimulated with each repetition. As much as we love chocolate, if we eat it every day at all times, it will cease to produce the same level of pleasure that it did initially.

The same thing happens with possessions. We long to have our own car, but once we have it, we want to trade it for a better brand or a newer model. If we love sneakers, having three different pairs is not enough, we always want the latest model. Going on vacation is not enough either, they have to be increasingly sophisticated and luxurious or they won't produce adrenaline.

Hedonist adaptation makes us adapt quickly to good things. As we accumulate, expectations rise, and that for which we have fought so much no longer gives us the same satisfaction as before. To obtain the same level of pleasure as we did in the initial experience, we need to increase the dose of that which gave us satisfaction, and therefore more money.

And having to earn more money in order to spend more money comes with significant personal costs: less time with the family, anxiety, stress and debt, among others.

The situation described leads us to feel progressively less free. The only thing left for us to do is to keep buying things to placate the anguish produced by withdrawal. We believe that the void will be filled that way, but all we fill is the physical space, since our emptiness is spiritual.

Eckhart Tolle[28] thinks that the great liberation from materialism comes with acknowledging our own ego or that "false self" that we have created ourselves to feel protected against the world's aggressions. According to him, the driving force behind the ego's behavior is always the same—the need to stand out, to have power, to get attention and own more. Besides, the ego is never self-sufficient, it always wants something from the others or from a given situation. It used people and contexts to get what it wants, but the gap between what it wants and what it has is never closed. And so, it becomes a constant source for restlessness and anguish.

In our culture, to live in order to own more things is an everyday reality which has become the norm for a lot of people. Life is seen as a hassle, and we live constantly solving problems, hoping to reach one day a longed-for happiness that never comes.

We will come back to this later but dealing with this "other self" or "shadow," which we all have to an extent, is no simple thing.

Can Money Buy Happiness?

An advertisement from Mastercard's credit card was fixed in the minds of many who, like me, probably remember it to this day. It said: "There are some things money can't buy. For everything else, there's Mastercard." Wise words.

Happiness can't be bought, that's for sure, but that doesn't mean that the way we invest or spend our money can't have an effect on it. In fact, if we spend it in sharing experiences with others or trying to improve other people's lives, then our happiness will likely increase[29].

This hypothesis can be confirmed by observing the sustained increase for the past fifty years in philanthropy and other altruistic endeavors, as well as business ethics and new ways of doing business where there's an awareness of the impact generated. Examples of this are The Giving Pledge movement[30], triple impact investments, social investment funds, B enterprises and ethical banks, among others.

Given that we have no way of accurately measuring the extent to which altruistic actions increase our levels of happiness, it's difficult to prove that the previous statements are true. Instead, money is a much easier parameter to measure. For example, it's easier to calculate the value of my house based on its sale price than on the well-being that living there generates for me and my family. The same thing happens with work: it's easier to evaluate a job offering considering the salary than the human quality of our future peers. And we have been led precisely by this sort of simplistic analysis to measure success, happiness and life in general through money.

But what would happen if we could measure our health levels, how much our friends love us, or the quality of our love relationships? Would we admire those who have higher indicators for those attributes, or those who have more money?

Let's imagine for a second the follow scene. A group of former schoolmates, now in their mid-sixties, meets to share and review their lives, promising each other to be absolutely honest. For purposes of this exercise, we're going to assume that the important attributes for our well-being are numerically quantifiable on a scale that ranges from zero to one thousand.

The reunion starts and these are the conversations that take place:

1) **Caesar, businessman, married,** the happiest of the group, tells his friends he feels completely fulfilled. He has four children and ten grandchildren. With his savings, plus what he got from selling his minimarket, he bought some land outside the city. His family visits him there every other weekend. Besides,

during the summer they all stay with him and his wife for a full month. Every Thursday morning he hikes up the hill with a group he has, and he actively participates in the programs for seniors offered by the neighborhood council. Caesar's health is in perfect conditions, and so he is planning to get a job.

2) Esther, engineer, single, used to be the most flirtatious and interesting person of the class. She had a brilliant career in a multinational cosmetics company. She couldn't have a stable relationship because her job had her constantly flying outside the country. She tells her friends that two years ago she finally decided to adopt two Haitian brothers. They were five and seven years old when she received them. Motherhood filled her with vitality, and that was the beginning of a different life, full of activities and new friendships. They take turns with the other parents to pick up the children at school, religiously go to a happy hour every Thursday evening, and every so often organize a trip abroad. In addition to this, for a few months she's been part of a running group, in which she met a younger man. Although she felt shy, she said yes when he asked her out. Now she is actively searching for someone to help her with her children, since the hernia in her back makes it almost impossible to keep up with them.

3) Raphael didn't finish school, since he chose to start a business instead. He's a very good friend but can be a bit arrogant, which is why whenever it's his turn to speak he doesn't skimp on details that everyone already knows from the press: that his retail empire continues to expand, and that he'll open new stores in Peru. Every time there's a new list of the wealthiest men in the region, his name is on it. From time to time, pictures of his properties in New York or Milan appear in home decor magazines. He's been married and divorced three times, and recently got engaged with a woman thirty years younger. He says he doesn't want any more children. He has more than enough with the five he already has, who only call when they need money. He adds that what bothers him is that they're not committed to the business; he is seriously thinking about threatening to cut them off if they don't start behaving in a serious manner. Next month he will have to travel to Atlanta for a check-up, since his diabetes keeps getting worse and he has a rather bad prognosis

Now that we know their stories, let's see what the well-being results are for each of them, taking into consideration only what was said during the reunion:

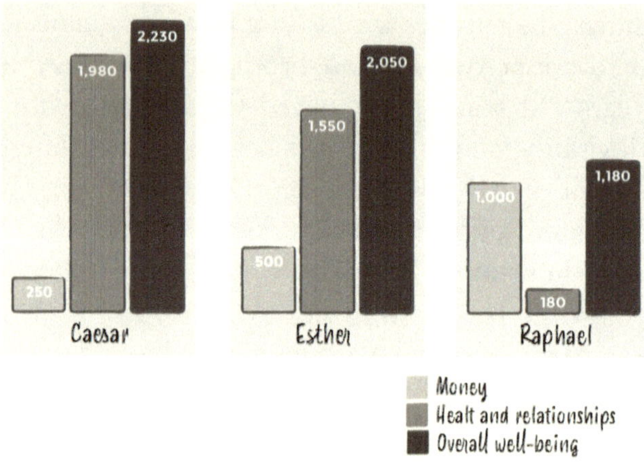

If we only look at the money indicator, Raphael has undoubtedly the most desirable life. But if we add health and relationships, the scenario changes completely: Raphael wouldn't be as admired, Caesar and Esther would almost double his well-being.

Do we really need a quantitative measurement to realize which life is better for us? Can't we come to that conclusion by knowing ourselves better and using our consciousness to guide our decisions? Perhaps later we will be able to answer this question.

Now What?

I was very happy to be finally able to answer several of my questions. The big "why" of life seemed a lot clearer, and I felt that, more than anything else, the happiness that I was looking for looked a lot like *Eudaimonia*.

Although I felt this progress, I also had the feeling that this was just the beginning. If the happiness I was looking for couldn't be reached by having money, power and fame, what was I supposed to look for? What did Aristotle mean when he referred to a happiness of the soul? It all seemed to indicate that I was about to discover a new world, completely unknown to me. Something less rational and more spiritual was about to come my way.

Existential Vacuum

> *Life is never made unbearable by circumstances,*
> *but only by lack of meaning and purpose".*
>
> Viktor Frankl.

Until this moment, I had managed to understand that there was a gap between the way I was living and the one I needed to live in order to feel complete.

During a family lunch (so typical of a Saturday) I told my sister-in-law, a psychologist, about this emptiness I was feeling. She told me I should read Viktor Frankl's Man's Search for Meaning[31]. She thought it was weird that I hadn't read it, since it's an all time classic and an important chronicle for Jewish people. Feeling ashamed, I read it immediately.

Viktor Frankl (1905, Vienna), neurologist and psychiatrist, was a Holocaust survivor. In his book he narrates his experience in Auschwitz, where he was subjected to hard labor, torture, starvation and being separated from his family, besides witnessing countless deaths.

Unlike most in his situation, Frankl survived. When asked how he managed to endure so much suffering and for so long, he alluded to his ability to hold on to what's really important in life: his purpose. For those misadventure companions who failed to survived, he coined the term "existential vacuum," which he describes as a heartbreaking feeling that makes life meaningless. A place where there is only suffering and a disconnect with the outer world, which takes away the strength to cling to life.

The situation described in the book is one of the most extreme I've ever heard of. That heartbreaking feeling he describes, when there's no hope or reason to live, seems to be the end of existence, and not death as might be expected. On the other hand, he suggests that when we have enough powerful reasons to want to live, what happens on the outside doesn't matter much because our soul, spirit, inner flame, energy, strength, however we wish to call it, will never go out.

Despite the obvious differences, as I was reading his autobiographical account I couldn't help but feel identified with that existential vacuum felt by those who didn't have a reason to cling to life. It was different for me. I had many reasons (my daughters, my husband and my family, without a doubt the most important part of my life) but I still felt that vacuum. To me, that feeling was a sign that there was something else to live for.

It was a vacuum that was intimately linked to the gap in my happiness that I kept feeling. A distance that had more to do with a spiritual need than a material one. As if an abyss stood between those two dimensions. Frankl made me learn that the spiritual need I felt wasn't there because I was particularly special. He says that human beings are not just biological, social and psychological beings, but also spiritual beings capable of transcending physical limitations through purpose of life and spirituality[32].

But what was the meaning of this spiritual dimension of the human being? I was having a hard time understanding it. It made sense to me that there was something else, even if we couldn't perceive it through the senses or understand it through reasoning. It's not something that I have fully incorporated even to this day, but there was a dimension, somewhat hidden, that didn't have to do with religion or anything I knew from before.

Reading different authors, I came to the notion of "Oceanic Feeling," which has been, for me, the most eloquent definition when it comes to understanding our spiritual plane. Romain Rolland, the 1925 winner of the Nobel Prize in Literature, coined the term while corresponding with Sigmund Freud almost a century ago[33]. I heard (but haven't been able to confirm it from an official source) that he used this term to refer to the following analogy: "just like a drop of water in the ocean, we are one with the whole, every person is a drop and the ocean is the universe."

In each of us this feeling manifests itself as the perception that the borders between the self and the world are diluted, even if for an instant. This fusion allows us to capture the world as an organic, interdependent and beautiful totality in itself. We have a hard time noticing this unity, since we rely on our senses too much, but the universal consciousness[34] can't be perceived through the senses nor understood through reasoning. We must add to this that we live hectic lives that prevent us from having the peace needed to feel the connection between all existing things.

Although the way to achieve this unity is highly complex, and is beyond what I'm able to share, we'll see later on (when we develop the concept of transcendence) that one of the ways to reach it is through our actions, our right way of living and relating to others[35].

I Was Not the Only One

I shared my emotions with others in different classes or talks about purpose, and found many people that, like myself, felt an emptiness. They also didn't understand why they felt it or how to fill it. In general, these were people who, at least in appearance, were set for life. However, they hinted that "something" was also missing.

Let's see some examples:

Summer, 45 years old. Dermatologist, married 15 years, 2 children:

"I'm a happily married woman, mother of two. I've been blessed with good health and financial stability. I'm looking for ways to satisfy an unsettling feeling that I have. It's like a void in the center of my soul".

James, 35 years. Corporate lawyer, divorced, one child:

"I have done everything by the book. I have a career that I've built for many years, and I make a decent living. But there's a restlessness inside of me that tells me there's more to life than this".

Andrew, 24. Commercial engineer, single:

"I'm trying to give my life some direction, a sense of purpose, something that will define who I am. I need something more, I don't want to do what others expect me to do–but I don't know how to get there".

Frank, 60 years. Real state agent, married twice, four grown children, recently became a grandfather:

"I've been happy, I can't complain. With a lot of effort, I've had a successful life and I'm very proud of that. But I feel I should leave my children and future generations something else. I wonder, what will my legacy be? What will I be remembered for? What part of me will transcend?".

Brenda, 36 years old. Architect, married, one daughter, from a deeply religious family:

"I've always considered myself a spiritual person. I believe in something superior, but I don't feel like I can find my raison d'être in religion. I would like to live my spirituality in connection to others and through my actions. I feel that we live in a fragmented universe, and purpose is a path to achieve

the union of our souls with the All. But I don't know if this is possible".

***

Trying to find patterns or clues behind this shared crisis, I couldn't help but notice a couple of things: we were all sort of less in an adult stage of life, and had our lives were reasonably solved. Let's delve into these coincidences.

Stages of Life

Paying close attention to the moment in life in which this void appears, it seems that the desire to search and live a life of purpose evolves in conjunction to developing our own identity[36].

While people can develop the need to find purpose at any age after twelve, it can only become an intentional search once identity consciousness has been formed. In modern societies, this happens generally during early adulthood[37] (between the ages of twenty and forty). This seems entirely logical, since it's hard to direct yourself towards what you want to become without first knowing who you are[38].

In the mid-adult stage (between the ages of forty and sixty) this intentional search that comes from questioning or being genuinely worried about our legacy to the world and the future generations can be reactivated[39].

Human Needs

The level of satisfaction regarding our most basic needs also matters when it comes to awakening this interest in purpose of life. As Maslow well puts it, if survival needs are not met, the only objective in life will be to focus on them. Indeed, if we're starving or lack a roof over our heads, our energy will understandably be placed on improving these deficiencies.

Roy Baumeister, social psychologist who has dedicated part of his career to studying purpose, claims that people in desperate situations are not under the right conditions to reflect about the meaning of life. When survival is at stake, purpose of life becomes irrelevant. The author states that this search becomes a dilemma for those who can take survival, comfort, security and a certain degree of pleasure for granted[40].

In this book I will not try to understand when a need is totally or partially met, since that's rather subjective[41]. The truth is that, as Frankl says, even if we must always struggle to survive, we should also ask ourselves: "what for?" We seem to have more means to survive, but fewer reasons to do so[42].

To sum up what I was saying, despite the crisis of purpose (or, why not put it this way, the beginning of an awakening) usually appearing in early adulthood, when our most basic needs are met, not everyone in this situation goes through it necessarily. In fact, according to Bronk, only a small proportion of the population awakens to the needs and concerns of living a life with purpose[43].

According to the most recent studies, thirty percent of the population show a desire to live a life of purpose at the onset of early adulthood[44]. These numbers go up to forty in the subset of those that are within the working sphere[45]. In the case of young people, only twenty five show this same desire[46].

Don't Let Fears Interfere

In a study titled "What Should I Do with My Life?", American writer and journalist Po Bronson chronicled more than nine hundred interviews to adults finding their purpose in life.

Bronson found out that fear is a recurring theme preventing people from walking the path to purpose. He gathered the four main reasons in his study, and they were all related to fearing something[47]. Let's see what they are and how they would look like in real life.

1/ Fear of not being able to discern between a true purpose in life and an apparently selfish desire.

Justyna, after graduating from Medical School, finds out that her real vocation is to become a pianist. However, following that path would mean abandoning everything she's ever done until that moment and letting down a cause that she has embraced for a long time. She would have to start from scratch to pursue her passion.

2/ Fear that this search will drive them away from loved ones instead of getting them closer.

Rayén, family mother, is a young and talented silversmith. Her silver jewelry is highly valued in the international market. A group of young Mapuche investors from California suggests that she moves to the US to give her production an international projection. Rayén finds the idea appealing, since she knows that the value of her jewelry would multiply ten times. However, out of fear of leaving her family behind, she doesn't even answer the phone.

3/ Fear that this search won't lead to practical results and will cause poverty instead of personal and economic growth.

Max studied Literature and Journalism, and always dreamed of becoming an editor. But when his friend Valentina asks him to invest so they can start their own publishing house, he thinks he'll end up losing all of his savings. He decides to keep his job as a journalist instead of taking a chance.

4/ Fear of seeing purpose of life as something mysterious and scarce, instead of concrete and generous.

Nikolay, a technology entrepreneur, is an atheist. Every time someone talks to him about transcendence or spirituality, he replies that that kind of thing isn't meant for him, but for holy people like Mother Teresa of Calcutta or the Dalai Lama. When his wife invites him to a meditation and self-awareness workshop, he says that he doesn't understand the benefits of isolating from the world, and that he thinks that it would be more productive to invest that time working and then giving to charity every so often.

> *Daring greatly is being brave and afraid every minute of the day at the exact same time."*
>
> Brené Brown

It would be interesting to find out what those who feel that void or need of purpose in their lives do.

At this moment, an exploration stage begins. As we'll see in the next chapter, it can start in different ways.

CHAPTER V

Starting a Path

> *Turn your gaze to the sun, and the shadow will remain behind you"*.
> Persian proverb.

Every path has a beginning, and that of purpose is no exception. I don't rule out that there are others way, but we will delve into the most common ways of starting our own path to purpose:

1. Active Search

The most frequent way of starting it is through an active search. This applies to all of those who decide to take control over their lives and not rest util they have filled the void that afflicts them. It consists, as the name indicates, in proactively taking responsibility about finding our path. The first step is observing, searching and experimenting with new opportunities and contexts that might seem attractive to us and that spark our curiosity. This style is typical of those people who show initiative, are extroverts, curious, and open to explore new experiences while seeking clear objectives[48].

It's a gradual trial-and-error exercise, in which we explore activities, groups of friends, jobs and, in general, any sort of novel experience. Virtues such as solidarity, collaboration and altruism can open doors so that we have new experiences that allow us to get to know ourselves better and recognize the activities and scopes that might be of interest to us. For instance, volunteering for some social project, or participating in communal activities at school, university or neighborhood, helping a family or a friend with their business or start up, are all situations that can help us activate our own search. Traveling can also be a great opportunity to open our minds and knowledge to other ways of living and conceiving life.

This process is born from the inside out, out of our own necessity and interior maturity. It can't be forced or imposed to those who are in a different stage or moment in life. Therefore, the desire to explore has to come out of our truest intention; it requires determination. It's also necessary to have the conviction to want to live a life of purpose, no matter how long it takes, and even if we fail trying, and even if those around us make us feel like idealists or wish to convince us that our efforts are simply not worth it.

During this search, it is common to reevaluate our affections (friendships, intimate relationships), the things we study or the work we do. We will also rethink the way we relate to money, power, fame and all those preconceived notions on what's supposed to be understood by success[49].

To Have Experiences

The way to find that which brings meaning to our lives, that moves us from the deepest, requires a previous exploration of the world in which we live. A tour of our experiences that will reveal to us what we love doing, our strengths, the ways in which we can contribute to the world, and the values and ideals that we stand up for.

The word experience comes from the latin ex (outside) and perior (to try). Experience is, therefore, a relationship between the subject and the outer world. In other words, it's not centered in ourselves but in our perception of reality.

Experience implies a process of change or transformation. After an experience (good or bad) we will never be the same. We dare step out of our comforting certainties and venture into the unknown and novel. In order to do this, it's important to keep an open mind to new experiences, which presupposes an open attitude, free of prejudice, to life and whatever events might present themselves, living each experience with a spirit of tolerance, not wanting to end them in advance.

Warning: this search is not limited to those who wish to change the world. Most stories about searching purpose are about regular folks, like you and I. The only difference is that we want to take responsibility for our lives, contribute to something bigger, rethink traditional canons for success.

Inspiration

Often, this search will start by observing those we admire, people whose lives we wish we had, or that perform activities that we find attractive. Many times that test which basically comes from others, from those we think have a desirable life or worth imitating, will become an invitation to explore in that same direction. It can also happen that we admire people we don't directly know but whose work or activities we find extraordinary and make us feels a special consideration. When we admire someone we feel a mixture of attraction and devotion, and that leads us to recognize values and qualities from others that we would like to adopt for ourselves.

During the first eight years of my career, I had the opportunity to work with Ximena, a brilliant lawyer with over forty years of experience. She became an inspiration to me. She was the only woman in the office that managed to reconcile professional excellence and family life. She was never a partner because she chose not to be, but she was more than qualified. Instead, she chose to work shorter days so that she could spend more time with her children.

Besides being an excellent professional, she was undoubtedly the most beloved person in the whole office. She would never forget a name or birthday, and always had encouraging things to say when she saw any of the young professionals struggling. Ximena was more than an inspiration to me, she was a model, a pillar. Her example made me persevere while raising my daughters, and gave me the courage to request a reduction in my workday. She showed me that there were alternative paths to those followed by everyone else. Even better, that each person makes their own path.

After that stage of my life, my next step was once again inspired by a woman. The first time I had the privilege of participating in an activity organized by the Comunidad Organizaciones Solidarias[50] [Charity Organizations Community], I came across Alejandra, one of the most extraordinary women I have ever met. She created this community of foundations and corporations, and managed to position them across the country as relevant agents to society. Her conviction and professionalism, but above all her passion communicating and spreading social awareness around her, had me completely captivated. What she transmitted was so authentic that the possibility of not joining her initiatives was unthinkable.

Alejandra rekindled all the justice and solidarity dreams I had when I was teenager. She made me dream again and remember what had made sense to me once. Wanting to be like her motivated me in a way I never felt for any lawyer, judge por politician. I did everything I could to learn more about her projects. I was even lucky enough to meet her and share projects, hoping one day I could irradiate the same conviction and authenticity.

Inspiration Test:

- Have you ever met anyone that made you say, "I want that life for myself"?
- Is there any family member you respect and would like to emulate?
- Is there anyone you've ever seen or heard that made you feel everything they said made sense?
- Among your acquaintances, who do you associate with your ideal of success?
- Why do you admire that person?

- What's inspiring about them?
- Do you think you could set an objective and goals that will lead you in a direction that's similar to theirs?

2. Reactive Search

This search stems from a pain we've lived that brings us closer to death, directly or indirectly. It's the result of a traumatic event that creates a void in us, generally from that place of suffering, which changes our lives forever. This search can be triggered by the loss of a loved one, finding out that we suffer from a terminal illness, losing our jobs, going through a breakup, having to migrate to a different country, the birth or suffering of a child. These experiences shake us so deeply that we end up reevaluating our priorities, objectives, goals, identity, values and everything that means something to us.

Different from what happens when our process is actively started, which posits a long process of trial and error, here the search starts abruptly and in a more radical fashion, since it doesn't involve a previous period of reflection—but rather a sudden painful stir that forces us to rethink ourselves.

It is no coincidence that many foundations that seek to solve our society's most pressing and painful matters were born after their founder or someone in their family went through some profound suffering. During that reactive search they were shown that the way to overcome suffering is by helping others who are going through the same misfortune.

Fundación Nuestros Hijos [Our Children Foundation] was created in 1991 aiming to assist children with limited resources suffering from cancer. It was born at the initiative of a group of parents who went through taking care or losing a child to cancer. They were seeking to replicate the care model received at St. Jude's Hospital in the US (world leader in treatment and children's cancer research), where treatment is completely free[51].

This can also be observed in the cases of Fundación Alter Ego, which treats children with cerebral palsy, and Fundación Complementa, for children with Down syndrome. Both foundations were founded by families whose members had suffered those diseases. Or Fundación Ganémosle a la Calle [Let's Beat the Streets Foundation], which supports children at social risk through sports, in memory of the founder's son, who was an outstanding athlete. Or Fundación San José, whose founder had previously adopted a child and sought with her project to help people going through the same process.

Carolina's Story

The death of Carolina's mother activated her path to purpose. Carolina was an exceptionally good lawyer, responsible, upright, hard-working, and had excellent relationships. In her senior year of high school, she had to choose between going to Medical or Law school. She would laugh at her own divergent interests. But she wasn't passionate about neither of them. To those around her, and to herself, it was clear that what she was passionate about was nature.

She worked as a lawyer for ten years, until one day her mother was diagnosed with terminal cancer. I remember the afternoon I ran into her on the street. We worked in the same building, but rarely met there. We sat on the sidewalk and she told me the news as she cried. The cancer was in a very advanced stage and her mother didn't have many months to live. She died soon after that.

This process transformed her and led her to question the true meaning of life. She would ask herself about the point of living half-heartedly when, at any given minute, the most important thing could just vanish. And also: how can we enjoy our lives now, each day, and not live as if happiness were to come only later?

Less than a year later, my friend dared to leave her established life and start from scratch. Only this time she started from her most authentic identity, from what she loved doing, even if that meant a smaller income, a loss in status, and a profession with less projection. She studied landscaping and started living her life of purpose: "Giving her love over through nature's nobility."

Shortly after, she was elected president of Chile's Club de Jardines [Garden Club]. She is now one of the most prominent landscapers in the country. And most importantly: she's a happy and self-fulfilled woman.

3. Hybrid Search (a little bit of everything)

The search can also happen in a hybrid manner. For instance, someone can have already started an active search when a traumatic event takes place, speeding up their process. And a source of inspiration can also stem from this event.

That's what happened to American television presenter Oprah Winfrey[52], who has always been closely linked to the spiritual world and who has confessed to be constantly reviewing her path to purpose. When she was thirty six years old she interviewed Truddi Chase, a woman who had been sexually abused during her childhood. As Truddi was narrating these episodes, Oprah felt touched by her guest's statements, to the point of thinking she would have to stop the recording. But she continued, even though Truddi's story provoked such an emotion in her that she could barely speak.

In subsequent interviews, Oprah has said that the story brought back endless traumatic memories from her own childhood that she had kept blocked until then. The successful woman from the communications industry had a precarious and rural childhood, during which she lived alone with her grandmother, since she had an absent father and her mother was forced to migrate to the city searching for a job.

One day, when she was nine, she went looking for her mother, but upon settling in the city she was raped and abused by relatives and close friends of the family systematically. When she was thirteen, she was sent to a juvenile detention center, and when she was fourteen she became pregnant but the newborn died in a premature delivery.

Oprah was motivated by these traumatic experiences to study and enter the world of mass media, where she would end up becoming one of the most influential people on television. As she has stated in many interviews, what she went through as a child made her feel the need to please others and never say "no" to them. She managed to give her life meaning by empowering people, especially young women, so that they could raise their voices and assert their rights.

Oprah Winfrey's story is a perfect example of a search that starts reactively. She builds her path through the traumatic experiences of being away from her mother and then abused. But once she decides to study Communications, her search becomes an active one. Finally, Truddi's story, in conjunction with her own, motivates her to struggle for women's rights.

* * *

I knew that I was searching for a spiritual type of happiness, and that lacking one created the void I felt. I also knew I wasn't alone in feeling this, and that there was a path to help me get started. I won't lie, getting to this point was a big relief for me. Little by little, I was finding the answers I had been searching for so long.

As I persevered in my search I could see clearly that purpose wasn't a unique mission for life, but rather a path towards happiness, which is not just made out of sensorial pleasures but also of something much more complicated to obtain.

However, as I progressed and answered some of my questions, new ones began to emerge. As if the greater the knowledge, the greater the doubts. Now I had to find out perhaps the hardest thing of all: **how to design a path that I had already started, a path that would have to guide me towards happiness.** This whole purpose thing seemed to be making me see life under a different light. As if I were starting on a new life philosophy. But I needed a plan, a roadmap...

PART II:
TELOS, A METHODOLOGY TO DISCOVER YOUR OWN PATH TO PURPOSE

Telos is an original methodology that I designed, which seeks to offer a holistic model so that you can design your own path to happiness.

I've named it *telos*, the Greek word for happiness (τέλος), in honor of the greatest philosopher of all times, my great guide throughout this path: Aristotle[53].

The Path To Purpose

> *Walk slowly, do not hurry, for the only place you have to reach is yourself"*.
>
> J. Ortega y Gasset.

Changes started at the beginning of this transformation path. To my surprise, I didn't feel like a different person. In fact, more than ever I felt like myself. But my priorities changed, no doubt about that, and life started looking slightly different. I didn't care about the same things as I did before, because they didn't make me happy anymore.

Now it was clear to me that the race for success, which had drawn me for years, was over. Or maybe it had never started for me. It was time to reformulate the typical goals imposed by society and discover those that were really my own. I wanted to feel free, no longer a prisoner to what others expected of me. I wanted to dedicate all my time, and not just a part, to that which really meant something for me and which I enjoyed. And that led me to a new way of seeing and living life, which required a lot of courage, effort and responsibility, and for which I was absolutely willing to risk myself.

During this process, purpose became my partner, my goal. But everything I had read so far seemed inconclusive. It was enough to enchant me, it didn't explain what it really meant and it didn't quite explain that I was applying it in my life. That's why I decided to create my own methodology (based on science, what I had studied and my personal experience), a holistic, coherent one that would allow me to shape my own path to purpose.

Trying to put together all these findings in my mind, I understood that the theories I had studied weren't incompatible with each other. I understood that, while we have a shared immutable purpose for all of us (happiness), in order to reach it we must each set different objectives and goals that will guide us there.

My starting point truly came when I fully eradicated the belief that there is a single purpose that lasts a lifetime, and that it differs for each human being. I felt that there could be more than one path to achieving purpose, maybe even many that change over time, as we evolve.

A Path of Life that Starts but Never Ends

Having the ability to live a purposeful life, aware of the reason behind our existence, is a uniquely human trait that never fades away; that is to say, it possesses infinite potential. We can always be happier. At the same time, since we never fully reach it, the challenge of keeping it alive is always present, whether it is to keep the same level of happiness or to try to make it greater. The important thing about it being a path or a constant process is that, when we go through it, we must not search for a final result—it's not something that you only get once. **The art lies in enjoying the path.**

The same thing happens with other values that we long for, like love. Love comes from our capacity to give it and for that fact alone we feel overwhelming joy when we love and give ourselves to others. We can always love more and be happier, which is why we say it is infinite, not a point you reach and that's it[54].

Just as loving our first child doesn't exhaust our faculty to love those to come, moving towards an objective oriented to purpose doesn't automatically mean we have achieved it in itself. The path doesn't end there. Each goal achieved moves us to the next. The apprehended object doesn't constitute this faculty; the ability to seek for it does. Reaching purpose isn't what makes us flourish. We become truly happy because of the path we travel .

This path starts with our intention, that is to say, a wish brought into action. And it progresses towards the one or several objectives we set, which we wish to make real but at the time don't exist. The goals that guide our path to happiness will be somewhere along the journey, between these two moments.

Why do we waste time wishing for something we can never fully achieve, like happiness?
Why not limit our objectives to the things within our reach?

The philosopher Robert Sokolowski[56] reckons with this concern, explaining that we need this type of desire because it provides a context that's beyond our practical world. It is a sort of frontier that we set for ourselves. It would seem that, in order for us to define wishes that can be fulfilled, we need those that can't.

Our rational appetite needs to extend itself beyond the realm of what's achievable so that it can define the region where it can be effective. For example, let's take a look at the Bill Gates Foundation, the biggest in the world. Its mission is to eradicate poverty from the planet, although its founder knows that at least in his lifetime that's impossible. However, this "impossible" wish has served as a vision for all of the important projects that the foundation carries out.

This type of wish, as useless as it may seem, reveals our most properly human kind of rationality. Wishing the impossible, as Sokolowski says, is not only a "going beyond" that we can't avoid; we wouldn't want to live without it.

Next, we will delve into intention, objectives and goals. We will use them as a framework and methodology to design our own path to purpose.

Intention: The Cause

Intention is a type of deliberation that precedes our decisions, and it is always accompanied by a cognitive process, or a process of personal reflection, that invites us to act. Our intentions lead us to prefer one thing over others. And, when it is right, it is morally oriented towards our ultimate goal: happiness. Knowing what's important and what drives us to try and reach the objectives and goals we set for ourselves means delving into the real reasons behind the things we do. The cause is the principle of action for our objectives and goals. Each time we ask ourselves, "why do I do what I do?", "why is it important for me to do this?", "what am I so enthusiastic about this?", we're investigating our intention.

For instance, if I choose to marry my boyfriend, it's important that I know the intention that motivates me to do it: is it because I wish[57] to love him for the rest of my days, or because I know he's a good man and will treat me well during our marriage? Likewise, when I perform an altruistic act, for example a donation: do I do it so that I can pretend or show off to others, or because I have a genuine interest in helping?

Delving into this intention will be decisive for my path to happiness, no question about it. This isn't something that we do often, but as we will see it is essential for a life of purpose.

There came a moment in my life when I asked myself why I was a lawyer, and if I wanted to continue being one. I wanted to know if I was motivated by passion or by something else. I realized I had no idea.

We often set important objectives for our lives without even exploring their cause, that is to say, without being fully aware of our decisions. In those cases, highly likely there will be an inconsistency between who we are and the things we do[58]. In fact, in numerous occasions we are not even able to foresee the future emotional effects of the things that are happening to us at the moment[59]. Living that way is to live in inertia. When that happens, our actions aren't motivated by a conscious intention but rather by an "automatic pilot" or, as psychologists would say, the subconscious.

I've talked to some people about the importance of intention, who think that the foundation on which a objective or goal rests is not important as long as the subject reaches those objectives or goals and feels competent and effective in the process. However, throughout this book we will see that this utilitarian outlook doesn't work for the path to purpose. To the point that **I can assure you that objectives and goals (of which we will go in depth later) we set will benefit us in terms of mental health, general well-being and personal growth, but only as long as there is a consistency between them and our intention**[60]. Only a reason that comes from our authentic intention (and not the ego's) unleashes the magic that we seek.

How can we know if we're facing an objective motivated by a real intention or the ego? In general terms, our intention can be motivated by love and moral responsibility or by fear and the seek for hedonic pleasure. The first one is basically our authentic intention, while the second, is more our ego talking.

Let's see some guidelines:

Objective motivated by an authentic intention	Objective motivated by the ego
Based on the truth	Based on pretending
Wants to collaborate	Wants to compete
Longs for the common good	Individualistic
Enjoys the path	Only interested in the result
Wants to understand their surroundings	Wants to blame others
Knows how to forgive	Resentful and vengeful
Grateful	It's never enough
Humble	Wants to feel superior
Spiritual purpose	Material purpose
Altruistic	Selfish
Accepts themselves and others	Driven by self-denial and intolerance towards others.
Motivated to do good	Motivated by power, money, fame and recognition.
Feeds on positive emotions, like joy and hope	Feeds on negative emotions, like anger and anguish.

The intention or the cause that moves us to achieve our objectives will determine if they lead us to our purpose. We'll see that discovering that authentic intention and its constitutive elements will be the key to this path. Which is precisely what we will deal with in the next chapter, when we develop the *telos* methodology.

The Objectives of Purpose: "P objectives"

We have previously discussed how complex human beings are. Because of this complexity, having a single purpose isn't enough for us to feel full. On the contrary, we usually need more than one, and we also need that all of them, individually and separately, lead us to a happy life, as if they were several routes leading to the same direction. These objectives allude to an envisioned future that doesn't exist yet. They refer to the world in which we wish we lived and for which we are willing to make sacrifices.

To classify these objectives that lead us to our purpose (or "P objectives," as we will call them) we will separate them depending on the sphere of life in which they take place.

Spheres of Life

Spheres of life are those spaces or activities in which we invest our time and energy. We could say it is the field where the game of life is played. In them, we put into practice our most relevant desires or aspirations.

There are several spheres, but we will focus on the most frequent ones seen in modern life:

> *1. Family.*
> *2. Spiritual life.*
> *3. Connection to nature.*
> *4. Recreational instances.*
> *5. Community life.*
> *6. Work.*

Let's see a brief description of each of them:

Family
When we talk about family, we do so in a broad sense. Family is a group of two or more people (usually tied legally, by blood or cohabitation) with a shared life project, with children or people in their care.

Family is one of the spheres that require more attention and energy. When children are also involved, it is no secret that their upbringing and education changes our lives forever, demanding of lot of dedication, responsibility and financial resources, so that each member can reach their greatest possible development.

Spiritual Life
Spirituality is acknowledging, accepting and embracing the fact that all living beings on earth are connected by a superior strength, and that our connection to others is based on love, kindness, compassion and solidarity, among other virtues. The need for spirituality in our lives manifests itself as a way of satisfying our desire to be united with the rest, beyond the physical part—a subject that we will explore when we discuss transcendence.

From ancient times, religion has been considered the only spiritual way in our lives. Big religions, by promoting the belief in a superior being, have helped individuals transcend their secular lives, encouraging faith in a life that goes beyond the historic, spatial and temporal coordinates of each individual[61].

Although religion has been the greatest source of spirituality throughout history, it's not the only one. In these times of hypermodernity, we are able to get to know different kinds of spirituality, like the oriental or others that have a secular nature. That's why when we speak of spirituality, it can be either religious or of a different kind.

Connection to Nature
Nature is a part of the vast universe of everything that can be found that isn't a product of human interaction. It relates to different kinds of living beings, like plants, animals and people. But also with all the elements that make up the natural landscape, like oceans, mountains, rivers, etc. Our interaction with the environment has seriously affected natural life on the planet, which is why several diverse movements that seek to preserve and protect our environment have originated.

Until a few decades ago, a life lived surrounded by nature seemed normal. Today it's a privilege only a few can afford.

One thing remains indisputable, though: for many of us, having direct contact with nature (touching the ground, climbing a hill, breathing fresh air) is fundamental to our physical, spiritual and emotional well-being. That's why the prospect of living a life that is somehow linked to nature has become a sphere in which we're willing to invest time and energy.

Recreational Instances
When we talk about recreation, we refer to the active use of free time for physical, emotional and intellectual amusement. It differs from leisure, which is a rather passive way of distraction, related to the easing and relaxation of mind and body. They share the fact that they are both unpaid and essentially voluntary.

Recreation helps us break with routine and everyday obligations, and relief accumulated stress, which in turn allows us to find a healthy balance between responsibilities and life pleasures. The recreational activities we practice can be related to sports or hobbies, artistic inclinations like music or theatre, and, in general, any active way of entertaining that isn't connected to our livelihood or main work.

The frequent practice of recreational activities brings us pleasant moments and a feeling of well-being and satisfaction, which is why we try to dedicate an important portion of our time to it.

Community Life
Community life refers to any voluntary unpaid arrangement of meeting with others, with whom we share interests and affinities. It can be a religious, political, ideological, civic, local or union group that seems important or gratifying enough to seek out and join. There are different ways of getting involved in public life.

We could also include in this sphere anything related to friendship. In *Nicomachean Ethics*, Aristotle states that friendship "is a virtue and is besides most necessary with a view to living. Without friends no one would choose to live, though he had all other goods[62]".

Work
Work is, most likely, the sphere of life in which most adults happen to meet. It is also the one we dedicate more time and energy to, since it is the main activity that allows us to pay for our living expenses. It can be a professional job or a trade, in the sphere of the arts or sciences or sports, it doesn't matter. For the sake of purpose, the important thing for us is to be alluding to our main activity and not a hobby or a secondary activity.

The needs that we seek to satisfy through our work, and that are important for our occupational well-being, can range from the most basic, like securing a stable income or a place where our physical integrity isn't in danger, to more spiritual ones, like generating a positive impact with our work.

In an ideal world, our jobs would reach a large number of people and help solve humanity's biggest problems. But that's not necessarily the case. We tend to think that that level of impact is the only one that matters, but in reality jobs with those characteristics are rather scarce, and we don't need to aspire to such magnitude to make a difference.

Just because they exist, every single job, profession or trade, is at the service of others. That reason alone generates a positive impact. That's just the way things are. If we fail to see that, it means that we haven't made a conscious effort. Purpose, then, can be found both in humanity's big causes and in more common and mundane jobs, since there is an implicit kindness in being of service to others.

Regardless of the type of work, studies show that those who perceive their jobs as a constant way of giving onto others, see them as a much more significant part of their lives than those who regard it as a mere transactional activity[63]. Neuroscientist Paul Zak distinguishes between "transactional" and "transcendent"[64] jobs to tackle this point.

Transactional jobs exchange goods and services for a price which satisfies both those who supply and those who demand. Transcendent jobs, on the other hand, have to do with the qualitative aspect of the service. They virtuously allow for us to fully achieve our capacities while also benefitting others. Which is why any job in which we can be of service to others has the potential to be transcendent.

Although any job has the potential to generate a positive impact, we can distinguish to kinds of impact: direct and indirect. Let's take a look at them.

1. Direct Impact

The impact is direct when the benefit generated in others or the planet is perceived by the doer without a conscious effort. It can be classified as:

Impact by Action:

We find this kind of impact in those who feel passionate about an activity to such a degree that they can only live their path to purpose by devoting themselves to that activity. We'll see this in more detail later when we go over the concept of passion, but it's basically the chef who can't picture his life without cooking, the musician who wouldn't stop composing, the tennis player who's always on the field, or the astronomer who keeps staring at the sky. Each of these people who are passionate about an activity can walk their path to purpose and generate a positive impact, as long as they share their activity with others. Whoever cooks or plays an instrument without sharing that with anyone else, cannot transcend. In sports, for example, this happens when you represent your team, neighborhood or country in a competition.

Impact by Creation:

There are also people who enjoy creating new things. That can mean innovating, finding solutions to problems, or undertaking a startup. Curious, bold and flexible-minded people can generate a positive impact, for instance, by finding solutions to existing problems, or by generating new jobs through their startups.

Impact by Contact:

Here, the activity or job is directly linked in time and shape with the benefit it generates, whether it be on people or the environment. There is a direct contact with the beneficiary, a person or nature.

A cardiologist who saves lives in a hospital knows what kind of contribution can be attributed to their job. Their actions are directly linked with the benefited patient, which makes the relationship between the job and the positive impact self-evident. The same thing happens with a psychologist in their office, or a teacher in the classroom with their students. It also happens to a veterinarian when they take care of an animal, or a park ranger with nature.

What's relevant is not the profession itself, but the possibility of having a direct contact with those who benefit from it. The leader of a group or business can also have that sort of direct impact upon the people working with him, by forming them, training them, inspiring them or giving them new opportunities for growth. Being a leader is an opportunity to positively impact other people's lives.

2. Indirect Impact

Indirect impact is harder to perceive, because there is a distance between the activity that is being performed and its final contribution. We are challenged to look beyond what's evident, to become conscious of the cause or value beyond our actions.

This kind of impact can be as beneficial as the direct one, or even more. However, since its connection with the benefit is not self-evident, it challenges us to be constantly connecting what we do with what motivates us. In fact, the way we identify an action, task or job in our minds can determine the sense and transcendence it generates[65].

In this sense, **levels of identification of an action** can be low or high. Low levels imply concrete, immediate and specific meanings. They are simple, tend to be automatic, regular and can be executed without conscious thoughts. For example, if for lunch I have meat and potatoes, when someone asks me, "what are you doing?", I'll answer, "I'm eating meat and potatoes."

On the contrary, high levels of identification take into consideration more abstract concepts that are further away from the action itself. Because of this, they allow us to evaluate our actions within a different context or a longer period of time. Because it is a complex exercise, this also requires a higher level of consciousness, one that allows for a self-definition in relation to inferior and more concrete objectives.

If we take the previous example to a higher level of identification, it would no longer be about eating the food in front of me. On top of that, I would evaluate other things, whether it's healthy, if there's enough to last me until dinner, if I would like to be accompanied by someone, etc.

The same thing happens in the mythical story of the cathedral. A passerby approaches a construction in progress and asks two workers separately: What does your job consist of?

One stares at him with a resigned face, and answers apathetically: "I'm putting a brick on top of the other."

The other one, with a look of glee, passion and pride in his eyes, say: "I'm building the biggest and most beautiful cathedral in the world. I might never get to see it finished, but I'm filled with pride because I know my grandchildren will pray here every Sunday."

In this story, we can appreciate how through the conscious process of identifying an action, the very same activity can have different meanings to those who do it. The first worker feels that he has a job, while the second has a cause, and moves forward in his path to purpose[66]. Both levels of identification are equally right, but their impact on how we perceive the transcendence of what we do is radically in opposition.

Those who use a low level of identification for their actions, experience low levels of satisfaction. On the contrary, those who achieve a higher level of consciousness, feel that they transcend through their job, because they're capable of associating it to their values and to the satisfaction of their most spiritual needs.

Nathalie Wilk, the founder of Culotte, left her job as consultant for a prestigious firm in order to sell safe and reusable women's underwear, especially designed for menstruation periods. At first glance, one might think that Nathalie is simply selling women's underwear. What kind of positive impact could she achieve if there are thousands of producers doing the same thing? When I talked to her, it became evident that the type of impact she generates, while indirect, is beyond a doubt.

– Me: Nathalie, a lot of people ask me how to generate a positive impact, or contribute to the world, by selling or commercializing products. Looking at you it would seem that it's possible.

– Nathalie: Indeed, I sell products, but that's just a means to achieve something else. With our product we are educating women in this country. We're hoping to break taboos around menstruation and people are grateful. It's a subject we don't talk about, and we have brought it to light by generating a community of women who feel much more comfortable and empowered about themselves. Besides, and this is a more personal view, I deeply relate with positively impacting our environment. We're crossing off tons of garbage with this solution.

    – Me: How do these changes in your work life make you feel?

    – Nathalie: I feel a spark of joy each time someone writes thanking us for having transformed an unpleasant experience with an innovative solution. I don't mind working more hours than before, packing and moving boxes, making deliveries—I don't remember another time in my life where I experienced greater fullness. I feel that there isn't a difference between who I am and what I do. There's an absolute consistency between my values and my actions.

What Nathalie has achieved with her startup is the challenge that small and large companies are taking up. When what we do has an indirect impact, we must appeal to the values that we seek to attain with our service. Building trust, taking care of the environment, improving the quality of our education, move forward with transparency, promoting justice and incentivizing diversity and inclusion—these are just some examples of the values that we, as citizens, want to promote, and that businesses know how to address. With this kind of impact in mind, thousands of companies are reviewing their business strategies, looking for ways of declaring their corporate purpose and attract talents that share their beliefs.

* * *

These spheres in themselves are no guarantee for a life of purpose. That is to say, having a family, a job or being in contact with nature, doesn't warrant happiness, but it allows us to organize for it. Our task is to find which of these spheres are really important to our happiness, and with that in mind, set the "P objectives" that will allow us to fully live them (since there can be more than one) and let them evolve next to us.

Our Values: What Really Matters

By choosing our "P objectives," what we're really doing is organizing our lives based on our values; that's what really matters.

From a social point of view, values represent cultural ideals. They are conceptions about what's good/desirable or bad/undesirable. They lie beneath social practices, norms and institutions, and they contribute to setting preferences, attitudes and behaviors that people see as legitimate or not.

They are hypotheses about how life should be lived, which determine if a result will be considered a success or a failure. For that reason, our values determine our behavior, the decisions we make and how we justify our actions. They also serve as criteria to select or evaluate people, their actions and opinions.

The relative importance given to the spheres of life is usually influenced by the cultural factor of the place we live in and the social groups we visit. Therefore, the amount of time and energy that we are willing to invest in each of them, and the relative importance that they might have in our path to purpose will be influenced mostly by the symbols that we have culturally acquired and that have been transmitted from generation to generation. This will influence, for instance, the value given to wisdom, the role of women and the balance between personal life and work.

American Factory, the 2020 Academy Awards Winner for Best Documentary Feature, shows that conceptions about the sphere of work can differ greatly between countries. In it, American and Chinese workers from a glass factory have a completely different perspective about their quality of life, despite doing the same activities within the factory. Americans seek to balance life and work, taking breaks during the workday and having relationships with coworkers, whereas Chinese see work as an end in itself, preferring to be away from their families and work on weekends than accessing any kind of enjoyment.

While society as a whole, and each individual on their own, possess a specific system of priorities they value, their influence on the way we behave is not always crystal clear. This is because a behavior or attitude usually involves more than one value, and between themselves values can complement or conflict with each other. For an individual, accepting a well-paid job with a future projection can be congruent with their values of success and material wealth, but perhaps will come into conflict with their values of independence and enjoying free time.

Values are tied to affection, which is why when a situation activates them, we are filled by potent emotions, positive or negative. It's hard to remain indifferent. For example, if I value truth, I'll get infuriated when someone lies to me. If I value diversity, I'll feel proud when same-sex marriages are legally acknowledged.

* * *

Exercise: State your "P objectives"
Once we are certain about our intention and the spheres of life that are key to our happiness, we must proceed to stating our "P objectives" (mentally or in writing).

You shouldn't start with the question, "What do I want from life?", since the answer here would be obvious and similar to most people: a big family, a never-ending romance with my partner, a job I love, hundreds of close friends, being radiant, having lots of money, helping the world, seeing all the countries in the world, being respected and admired by those around me.

We all want that, and no wonder. But as Mark Manson says, in his bestseller *The Subtle Art of Not Giving a F*ck*[67], the real important question, considered by few, is, "What things am I willing to fight or suffer for?" The answer to this question will help us decipher what's really important to us.

> *- Am I willing to work twelve hours a day to become a millionaire?*
> *- To spend four hours at the gym and not eat chocolate to look perfect?*
> *- To take care of my children when they cry or can't sleep at night?*
> *- To respect my partner and not evade difficult conversations?*

If we're willing to go through whatever it takes to reach our objective, that's because it's important enough to become a "P objective."

Eleven practical tips to state your "P objectives":

1/ Source of inspiration: your statement must mobilize yourself into being a better person.

2/ It's a cause; they originate as an intention. They must answer the question, "Why do I do what I do?", not a specific "what." We'll use goals to organize what we do. For example, I want to live my life accompanied with another person. That's my cause. For that to happen I might decide to live with my partner. That's my what or goal.

3/ Free and boundless: it's enough to have one objective in life, but we must not forget humans are complex beings, and frequently we'll have objectives in more than one sphere. Or more than one objective in a single sphere.

4/ Idealist: this is about our wishes, which don't answer to tangible or quantifiable methods. That's the realm of goals.

5/ Ordinary: you don't need a heroic objective. The path to purpose is not limited to the Dalai Lama or Gandhi. It's also for ordinary people, like you and me.

6/ Priority: if you're clear about your priorities amongst your spheres of life, even better, because this will let you make better decisions if there's a conflict between two or more of your objectives.

7. Challenging: it must make you expand your limits, get out of your comfort zone.

8. Active: these objectives must be present within our thoughts and emotions so that we can make them happen through our goals. Their success will depend on us taking them to the sphere of tasks. Therefore, some of these verbs will frequently be used to describe objectives: love, create, grow, develop, lead, contribute, serve, provide, collaborate, raise awareness, inspire, educate, heal, etc. They always depend on you, so they must be formulated positively, because that will confer them a sense of proactivity. For instance, "wanting to form a family" is not the same as "avoiding being alone."

9. It must be an end in itself and drive us to our happiness: this is a key aspect. We want our objective because it makes us happy and not because it's a means for another end that might *eventually* make us happy. For example, working to support my family doesn't originate an objective within the sphere of work, but would rather be, as we will see later, a goal within my family objective.

10. Evolve: objectives are not static, they will evolve next to your emotional, psychological and spiritual development. The important thing is that you think of them as having a continuance that allows you to seriously commit to them. In general they last years, decades or even a lifetime, when we set objectives that are impossible to fully tackle (ending extreme poverty, for instance).

11. Simple and easy: don't look for long and complex sentences. In the end life is about living and enjoying the simple things.

Some examples of "P objectives" statements based on life spheres:

Family	Establishing a rewarding loving relationship	Having kids and starting my own family	Taking care of my loved ones and staying always together
Work	Improving the qualify of life for sick people	Creating opportunities for the new generations	Connecting different people who could empower each other
Spiritual Life	Widening my level of consciousness	Reaching the knowledge of superior worlds	Trusting the creator's perfect plan
Connection to Nature	Protecting the world from climate change threats	Conserving and preserving natural resources	Making of nature an accessible good for everyone
Recreational Instances	Transmitting emotions through art	Exploring new places in the world and making them accessible to others	Achieving a balanced lifestyle physically, mentally, and spiritually.
Community Life	Contributing to the safety of young people in my community	Representing the rights of those without a voice	Fighting for my country's democracy

My first "P objective" is: ________________________________

____

My second "P objective" is: ______________________________

____

My third "P objective" is: _______________________________

____

Goals

Goals are short- and medium-term results that we want to achieve. They help us generate a life plan and feel that we're progressing in a determined direction. Setting them enables us to stay motivated in time and tackle each of its stages realistically, moving forward towards our objectives and purposes. In short, goals bring our everyday life closer to our purpose, since each of them directs our path to happiness.

The big difference between objective and goals is that the first seek to direct our lives and guide us along a long-term path. Goals, on the other hand, seek concrete and tangible results, and plan our everyday life within that path. Goals help us go from planning and thinking into action, which is one of the essential aspects of the matter at hand—**purpose always takes place in the doing.**

This combination is very efficient and rewarding. In my experience, when I started structuring my goals in terms of objectives, I started focalizing much better in the things I was doing, and whatever anxiety and anguish previously generated by the future started dissipating. Notwithstanding that goals are always facing the future, in a paradoxical way I stopped thinking about it and my attention shifted to the present I could control instead of the future I couldn't.

Perhaps the most surprising thing about this way of planning our lives is that when we conceive goals as part of a path or something bigger, we stop worrying about meeting them just to get them done or feeling successful. We are instead moved by the function our goals have in the path as a whole, in the Everything—and this allows us to chase them for the mere satisfaction of walking the path we have set for ourselves. If a project doesn't turn out as we hoped, we can only accept that and move forward with whatever comes next, because each goal is not evaluated in terms of success or failure but rather as part of something bigger.

As we set goals towards the same objective, we'll start finding that our actions are organized in a way that will make things flow much better. At the same time, a clarity will emerge that will push us forward to persevering and keeping our commitments despite obstacles, making sacrifices and staying on the chosen path with an unscathed will.

Tips:

1/ Goals for each "P objective" can be one or many.
2/ Must be stated in a tangible or measurable way.
3/ Must be short- to medium-term achievable.
4/ Must invite action, relate to that which you do.

Exercise: identify goals
Now we'll take three of the "P objectives" previously describe and identify their respective goals:

"P objective"	*Goals*
Having kids and starting my own family	1. Finishing my education. 2. Committing in a loving relationship. 3. Saving money to be able to cover our expenses.
Creating opportunities for the new generations	1. Finding a job in a company with a kindred purpose. 2. Professionally preparing for the next three years so I can reach young people's hearts. 3. Creating a team to design a first-class program to fight drug addiction.
Representing the rights of those without a voice	1. Participating in a political movement. 2. Generating strong bonds with the most needy communities. 3. Creating a communicational strategy to raise awareness about this cause. 4. Obtaining financing for the next two years.

Let's recapitulate what we've seen so far:

1. Our path must always have as its lodestar our purpose as human beings: happiness.
2. To be happy we must first discover and walk our path to purpose, unique to each person and constantly evolving.
3. This path sets a field of activity that starts with our intention and reflects on our "P objectives" that relate to our values, and goals that relate to our actions.

This path can be made out of different routes which in turn can be parallel or intertwine when a single goal works for more than one "P objective".

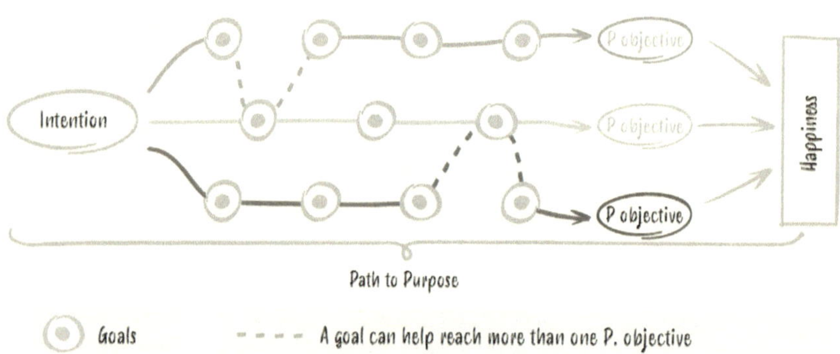

Path to Purpose

Goals   - - - - -   A goal can help reach more than one P. objective

With this in mind, we must invert the way in which we plan our lives at present:

Going from a traditional mentality:

Meet your **goals** ⟶ if you do, then they weren't challenging enough, so set yourself some new harder ones and you'll be **happy eventually** (which we know it's not true since we're constantly setting new goals).

To a mentally that fits your path to purpose, and invites you to live life thus:

Discover your intention, that which you genuinely desire, and find out what makes you **happy** ⟶ with this in mind, set your "**P objectives**" and use **goals** to make progress and enjoy the path. If you don't feel happy, something's not right.

↻ Check and reset your "P objectives".

> *The tragedy of life doesn't lie in not reaching your goal. The tragedy lies in having no goal to reach. It isn't a calamity to die with dreams unfulfilled, but it is a calamity not to dream...*
> *It is not a disgrace not to reach the stars, but it is a disgrace to have no stars to reach for.*
> *Not failure, but low aim is sin".*
> Benjamin E. Mays.

Personal Map

A great way of organizing and visualizing our growth so far is with a map that allows us to incorporate purpose, objectives and goals in our path to purpose.

Personally, structuring things this way has been enlightening. A few years ago I defined my own objectives, which are three, and I established a clear hierarchy between them:

1. Family: this sphere of life has always been the most important one for me. Since I was a teenager I wanted to have my own family. I was lucky to find the ideal man for me. Wanting to be a mother happened early and in a startling way.

These days, my "P objective" in this sphere is "giving my family all my love each day and in every detail, mutually supporting each other so that everyone can flourish and be fully happy."

2. Work: this sphere has been the most challenging one, and the one which made me research purpose as a way of focusing myself. For a long time, I was driven by inertia and properness, but now that I have abandoned the "auto pilot" I've been able to set my own objective.

My current "P objective" is "raising awareness about how important purpose is for people's well-being and companies' sustainability."

3. Spiritual Life: this is the most recent sphere in my life. The spiritual way was activated in me when I found purpose. And even though it's just starting, I sense it'll become much more prominent.

For now, and without the certainty of the other spheres, I would say that my "P objective" is "growing spiritually and acquiring higher levels of consciousness."

Once my "P objectives" were clear, I started setting goals that would get me closer to them. Or rather, that would spark life into them. Let me share my personal map with you:

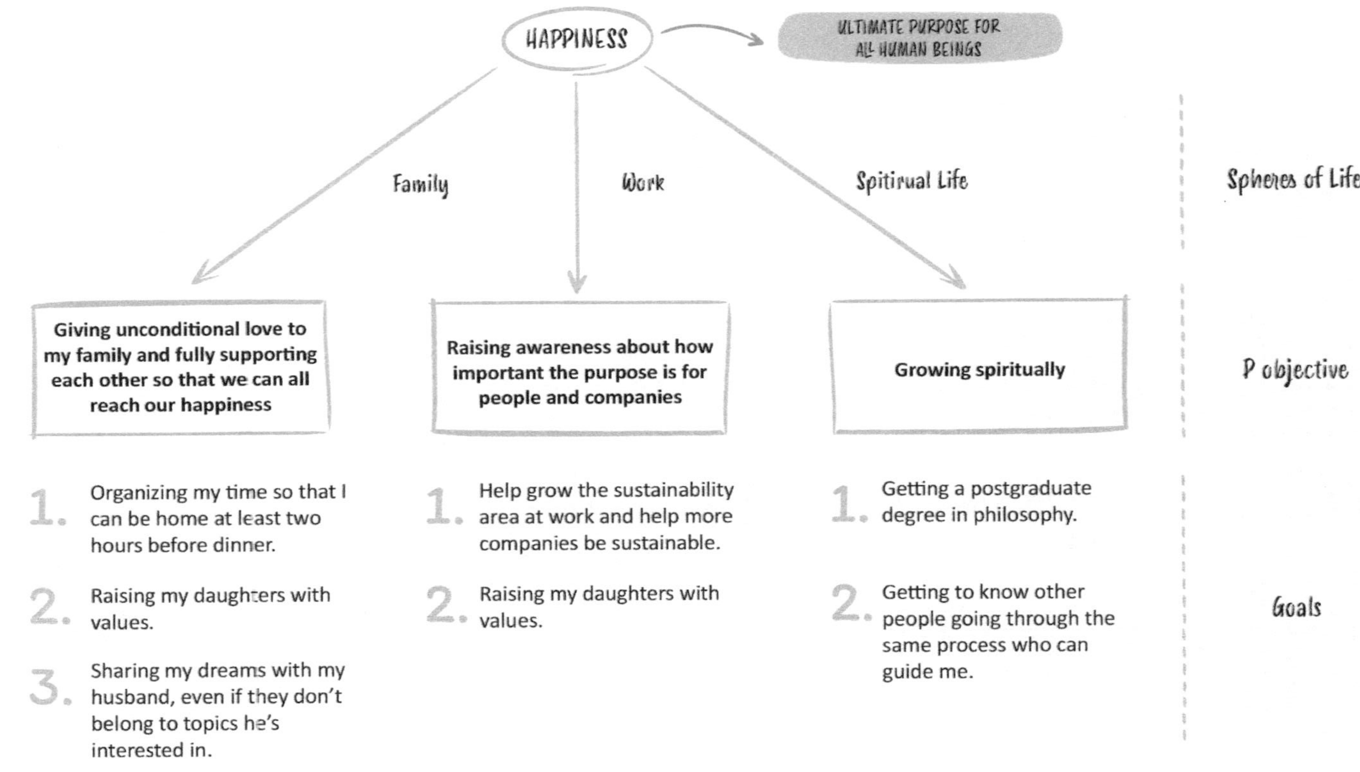
HAPPINESS
ULTIMATE PURPOSE FOR ALL HUMAN BEINGS
Family
Work
Spitirual Life
Spheres of Life
Giving unconditional love to my family and fully supporting each other so that we can all reach our happiness
Raising awareness about how important the purpose is for people and companies
Growing spiritually
P objective
1. Organizing my time so that I can be home at least two hours before dinner.
2. Raising my daughters with values.
3. Sharing my dreams with my husband, even if they don't belong to topics he's interested in.
1. Help grow the sustainability area at work and help more companies be sustainable.
2. Raising my daughters with values.
1. Getting a postgraduate degree in philosophy.
2. Getting to know other people going through the same process who can guide me.
Goals

Your Own Personal Map

Based on what we've seen so far, design your own personal map. It doesn't have to be finished yet. As we move forward, you'll be able to check if it's designed to contribute to your path to purpose or if it still needs to ripen.

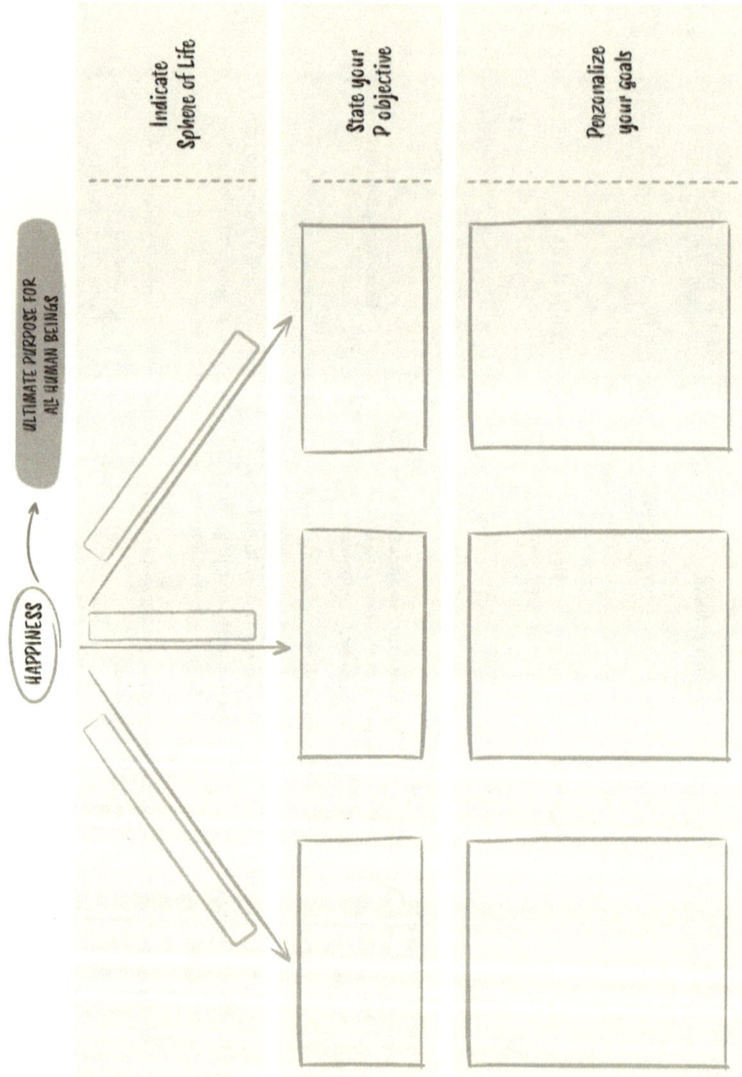

You can download copies of this Personal Map in www.sharonirosenberg.com

102

It's not easy to create our own map establishing objectives and goals. The tips and pieces of advice that we've given so far are just a starting point. So that we can confirm that this personal map contributes to our happiness, we must delve into the essence of purpose, that emerges from the intersection of two different dimensions:

· **The inner dimension: Who I Am.**
· **The outer dimension: My Place in the World.**

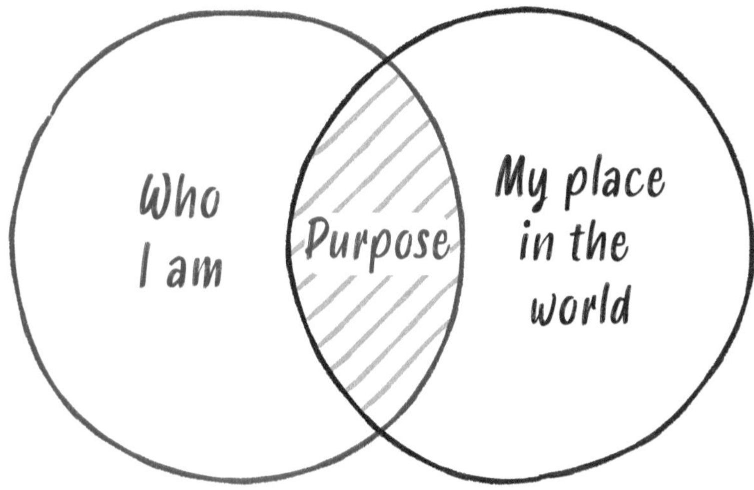

The inner dimension contains two elements, as follows:
Who Am I – containing:
· First element: *authenticity.*
· Second element: *passion.*

The outer dimension contains two elements, as follows:
My Place in the World – containing:
· Third element: *meaning of life.*
· Fourth element: *transcendence.*

If our "P objectives" are defined based on the previous four elements, we'll likely and progressively start feeling the three impacts of *telos*:

First impact: a transformation of the values that we consider important.

Second impact: we'll start living a highly motivating life and realizing that we're expressing all of our potential.

Third impact: we'll reach *Eudaimonia* or happiness, and we'll start seeing the world differently. We'll redefine our success model, and feel free, with a capacity for love unknown to us until then.

Each of the following chapters deals with one of these elements and their impacts, so that we can finally apply them to our personal map.

Who Am I?
Authenticity And Passion

The first step to setting our "P objectives" is knowing who we truly are. For that, we must start a process of self-knowledge, which will allow us to differentiate ourselves from other people and our surroundings, recognizing that we're individuals with our own singularity.

> *There are three things extremely hard: steel, a diamond, and to know one's self".*
> Benjamin Franklin.

First element:
Authenticity

Know thyself!

The Delphic oracle was a place of pilgrimage visited by great personalities of Ancient Greece seeking answers from the gods regarding their destiny. The words "Know thyself!" were inscribed (almost as a warning) at the entry of the Temple of Apollo in Delphi, reminding us of the importance of looking within before being looked at from the outside. These words were inscribed in gold, making it almost impossible to cross the threshold without looking at them.

The message was a call for reflection, to being aware that whoever wished for the oracle to share the messages of the gods with them, first had to work with their own inner self. In the room where the prophetess, a wise woman trained since childhood to reveal oracles, was, one could read the following:

"I warn you, whoever you are, Oh! You who want to probe the arcana of nature, that if you do not find within yourself that which you are looking for, you shall not find it outside either! [...] Know thyself and you will know the Universe and the Gods"[68].

This message, perhaps the most well-known from Ancient Greece, goes to show that the best questions come from self-knowledge. And that no question makes sense if we don't answer the most important of them all first: Who am I?

* * *

This inner search requires a personal process of reflection, introspection, and self-knowledge. Purpose invites us to explore and be curious about our roots, find inspiration in others, learn from our experiences and have as many of them as we can. While at first this can generate some anxiety or anguish, you'll be surprised when you realize that the search can be as challenging as it can be rewarding. And despite it being a process that we all start at one point in life, once it begins it never ends. We will always be, to a greater or lesser extent, searching or revitalizing our path to purpose, so that it's as true to ourselves as possible.

To discover that which is important for each of us, we must be willing to invest time and energy[69], since it requires a lot of space for reflection from us and the courage to take decisions that, at times, might destabilize us. It's advisable to share this process with someone else, someone we can express our emotions with. Often it's not until we put our thoughts and feelings into words that our perceptions and emotions become real. It can happen with a family member, a good friend, a mentor (as it was my case), the help of a psychologist or some sort of spiritual guidance.

Knowing ourselves, knowing which is our true identity, is the first step to knowing what kind of goals will make us live a life of purpose. Our authenticity separates us from the rest and makes each path to purpose different and unique. Having a true identity means recognizing yourself as the main character of your own life, in what you are and what you do, in what you think and say—and it also means finding out that which you are not and will never become.

Awareness of Our Own Identity

There's no other way of knowing ourselves than through our consciousness, which is the capacity of human beings to see and recognize themselves in their own identity. It reflects the knowledge that someone has of themselves, their thoughts and deepest reflections[70]. Being aware of who we are means an individual evolution that allows us to separate that which we think or want to be from that which we really are, with the positive and negative aspects that this brings.

Consciousness is that little flashlight that we place above ourselves that once is lighten up it allow us to see inside ourselves and all around. It helps us put the necessary attention into our actions and on to the intention that motivates them. When we observe the causes of our actions, the reason behind the things we do, the why of our behavior, we encounter with our true self. Thus, when we move away from the flow of our thoughts, from the content of our lives (what transpires) and from what our surroundings expect from us, we start a deep process of self-knowledge.

There is another side of it, that act as a personal moral judge. This faculty lets us see the full stage and allow us to see life in perspective, so that we can contrasts our own perceptions. Why is it so useful and necessary? Because we can't trust our own interpretation of facts. We're experts in justifying our actions and ruling in our favor, even when we're wrong. We want to believe that trust is the most important thing in our relationship, but as soon as we can check our partner's cell phone we do. We want to believe that we care about our health, but we pay little to no attention to our eating habits or doing sports. So we need this moral judge, and we need to listen to it, because it will give us the necessary for finding the consistency between who we are, what we do and the impact we can to create in the world.

This is no easy task, and you'll soon realize that it carries a great responsibility. By becoming aware of our intention and actions, we understand that the path to happiness depends fundamentally on us, and it's no longer possible to blame others for our failures or frustrations. On the other hand, we find out the importance of each decision made, because our path is forged by adding all of them. And sure, by holding ourselves responsible, we can't help but also take charge of the impact our actions generate in others and in the world around us.

As far as I'm concerned, for instance, I had no understanding of the damage the textile industry was doing to the environment until I saw the documentary The True Cost. Now that I'm aware of it (rather, that I chose to be aware) I've changed my consumption habits, finding out the origin of the things I buy and buying less.

Becoming aware is a path of no return. Once that flashlight illuminates our path, you can't have your inner light fall asleep again.

Levels of Awareness

Becoming aware is not an automatic process. One could say that there are different levels of depth, and the more we advance, the more aware we become. Renowned spiritual leader Deepak Chopra[71] has classified awareness in three levels:

State of Contracted Awareness	Here we find ourselves at the same level as our problems, which is why we can't solve or get out of them. We feel trapped, confused and internally conflicted, which raises our levels of frustration, diminishing our energy. Here we are always on the defensive and fearful.
State of Expanded Awareness	Solutions start emerging. We widen our vision beyond what's concrete. We start letting go of problems, connecting with others, gaining self-confidence, diminishing our internal conflict. We realized we've reached this state when we no longer feel stagnant, when we mobilize ourselves following our wishes.

State of Pure Awareness	Here problems seem to disappear, and each challenge is seen as an opportunity for growth. We feel completely aligned with nature and feel boundless. It demands that we're constantly open to the answers that present themselves.
	Our wishes are spontaneously satisfied. We know that whatever comes next is the best thing that can happen to us. We feel certain that the universe is our home. We see the world in a compassionate and understanding way.
	In this state we live a spiritual life that influences every aspect of our lives, finally fully understanding the concept of spirituality or transcendence.

The Ego

During this process, we must also become aware of our egos, as understood by Eckhart Tolle and Deepak Chopra. Both state that the ego is a false image built around ourselves to fence against the world's aggressions. This formulation differs greatly from that of psychoanalysis, which understands the ego as the awareness of the self.

Tolle claims that the ego is a construction we undertake precisely to avoid living the present in its full intensity, denying and running away from fear and pain. That way, the ego leads us to stare at what we want without actually getting involved with the present, let alone enjoy it . In other words, it builds a wall around our true identity, since at all times it tries to project a false image of ourselves.

Becoming aware of that ego allows us to recognize the things that we are not, thus eliminating the biggest obstacle in the way of knowing who we truly are. During this process we will realize that the ego is a fragile construct. By making it visible through consciousness, by recognizing it, by accepting it exists and dominates us, we also accept its limitations and avoid being controlled by it. The idea is not to repress it, drown it or deny it—but to embrace it and observe it without making any judgment. That's the only way the ego will surrender to consciousness, to our own authenticity, and lose its dominion over us.

110

Acknowledging Your Own Emotions

The word emotion comes from the Latin emovere (to move, transport, impress) and it is precisely something that takes us out of our usual state and moves us in a concrete direction.

The most basic emotions are fear, anger, revulsion, sadness and joy, and they can be classified as positive or negative. Negative emotions aren't necessarily bad, as their name might suggest. They exists so that we can sense that there's something wrong, and to warn us about our mistakes so that we don't repeat them. This type of emotion is a call for action, to change and improve things.

Emotions have a biological origin, as Charles Darwin demonstrated, and therefore are considered universal. Each time we feel one, our brain releases chemical substances that neurologically strengthen a experience, and that generate a change in us[73]. Then, when we realize this, we rationalize it as a thought or feeling.

Generally, emotions hide information related to a need that hasn't been fulfilled, reflecting certain aspects of the person who experiences them. Therefore, when we are aware of our emotions, it's as if we could read each interaction and experience between the lines, seeing how they resonate and leave a lesson for us. They allow us to distinguish between that which we like and that which we don't, enabling direct access to knowledge related to our own identity. For example, when something makes us feel anger or fear, we try to avoid exposing ourselves to that situation again, whereas we seek to repeat the ones that caused joy. In other words, they're like a GPS that guides us through our preferences.

Emotions are expressed through the body, but they also affect our mind, since they're amazing at anchoring memories. If something excites us, we will likely remember it in the future, unlike the things that make us feel indifferent, which we tend to forget easily. For that reason, they influence the way we interpret our past and, consequently, the way we behave in the present.

Emotions help us perceive and interpret the world from the most personal, and are also the vehicle that lets us relate to those aspects of our authenticity that we're not fully aware of. Sometimes we choose to repress them, pretending they don't exist. Not necessarily because we want to, at least not consciously, but rather because of social and cultural reasons that are contrary to our biological needs. For example, when we're afraid of expressing how we feel to those we're attracted to because we are afraid of not being reciprocated.

The important thing is to know that we are not dominated by our emotions, and that we can change the way we feel regarding certain situations once we're aware of them. As Aristotle says, emotions are deeply related to beliefs (an idea or thought assumed to be true) and, therefore, we can change what certain circumstances generate in us if we manage to change the beliefs we associate with them[74].

Throughout this path to purpose we'll have to be attentive to those emotions and let our consciousness analyze them as much as possible, so that we can see the cause behind each of them, negative or positive. This means letting them flow without repressing them, since that would mean not letting our inner light do their job. You'll see that, when we let them flow freely, we will find intentions, thoughts and feelings that we had ignored until then.

Ariela let her emotions flow and gave permission to her inner light to delve into her authentic identity. Let's get to know her story.

Ariela's Story

She was only five years old when she held a tennis racket for the first time. Her father liked this sport very much, so from a very early age, and together with her sister, they all started going to the club. After a few years, his father noticed a talent and he encouraged his daughters to train more often and play championships on the weekends.

112

When she was nine, Ariela won her first tennis tournament, and at eleven she was crowned Chilean champion in her category. She started travelling through the country, then attending South American tournaments, and finally touring Europe and the United States. When she was fifteen, she moved to Tampa, Florida, to a boarding school tennis academy. Its name was Palmer Tennis Academy, and around a hundred young people from all over the world lived there. They all shared the same goal: becoming number one.

She started feeling asphyxiated by sports performance, and the high expectations and demands put on her. Ariela felt like she didn't belong in that competitive world. She was far away from her family, her land and, deep down, she knew that she didn't like tennis enough to make a career out of it. Despite all of that, there were some bright things too: she got to travel the world, meet great people, perfected her English, and, above all, she felt she was part of something bigger. They were all the same in the academy, despite religion, nationality or social status.

That's the reason that kept her there all those years. The dream of becoming a tennis player wasn't hers, it belonged to her parents—but at that age she couldn't have known that. Let alone go against it and take another path.

For Ariela, training everyday was like going to school, and no kid ever questions that. She did fantasize about becoming an adult. She dreamed she would be fully happy, since she would be able to do anything she wanted and she would start her own family.

With the turn of the millennium, she quit tennis and before she turned seventeen she enrolled in Florida International University, in Miami, to get a degree in International Relations. His father wasn't very happy with the decision, since a career with that name doesn't even exist in Chile. She was also dating someone his parents didn't think was appropriate for her. That's why a year later her family decided she would return to Chile.

They promised her that, if she didn't adapt in six months, she could go back.

And that's how the best time of her life up until then ended. In college, she had made friends, had a boyfriend and the passion for studying had made her feel empowered. She was turning into a woman of character, with her own opinions and criteria. But once more she had to follow a path that others had traced for her. When she returned to Santiago, she found out she was already enrolled in the best university, to study that which was destined by birth: Law. At first, she tried to fight against it. She felt duped.

Adapting was hard, but she was lucky to make great friends in college, who made her feel at home.

She didn't dislike Law school, but it wasn't like on TV—there was a lot to memorize and little space for debating or contributing with new ways of building a fairer society. However, once again there wasn't any room for thinking. She had to go to college, hopefully to the most prestigious one, and study a traditional career, and get good grades, so that she could get a job in the best law firm. Now everyone was proud of her. She was fully complying with her duty.

Ariela didn't question any of this. She was happy. She was well received at home, her grandmother (her best friend) lived close by and some of her college friends became accomplices and life companions. Women with strong personalities and opinions, just like her. Besides, she found the perfect space for her to display her passion for the communal in a foundation. Soon after she met Alberto, a bright student of engineering and an athlete, healthy and charming. They shared the same traditions and he was also the son of one of her parents' best friends and associates.

She fell deeply in love. At first, she was reluctant to believe it: the easiest explanation was that she had fallen in love with him to please his parents. But her love was sincere. She never thought she could love someone so much, and that her love would become an energy that would move mountains. After four years of dating, they got married. And then there were new problems. One year after their marriage, their parents broke their partnership. Their long friendship became compromised.

This conflict eventually affected Ariela's relationship with her parents. They kept her away from the family for a couple of years, forcing her to take sides. It was either her family or her husband's. But this time she was an adult and she managed to distance herself from her father's grip. Her love for Alberto was so complete that it gave her the courage she needed. She was no longer her parents' adored little girl but became, in their eyes, "rebellious and disloyal." Her past had taught her that things were never perfect and therefore, while she suffered, it was the first time that she did what she thought was right.

Around that time, Ariela started working as a lawyer for the biggest consulting company in the country. And a couple of years later, her first daughter was born. The next year she had a second one, and, three years later, a third. Ariela felt her heart exploding with love. She finally had the life she always dreamed of, and was very aware and thankful for that.

But some time after that, she found herself, without wanting it, in a crucial life moment. One of those where you know that, no matter what happens, nothing will ever be the same. Things started unfolding as the day of her thirty-third birthday, which was also the day one of her daughters turned two, was approaching.

Ariela and Alberto had decided not to have any more children. Those wonderful prenatal and postpartum periods, when she could escape her "ideal" work life and seek shelter in her daughters, would then come to an end. Everything was seemingly going well, it was the best of worlds: she had a beautiful family, a very good marriage, and a promising career in one of the most prestigious companies in the country, practicing a profession that she herself had chosen and that it had taken her ten years to build.

She no longer felt the pressure to abide by her parents or other people. And yet she still felt like she had to satisfy certain standards or norms linked to an idea of properness. In other words, she was happy in her personal life, free in her decisions and content with her profession—but something didn't feel quite right. She felt a void she couldn't identify. Why?

For the first time in her life, Ariela started asking questions that she had never dared to ask herself when she was playing tennis, studying law, or when her parents interfered with her love life. Who was she? What was her place in the world? The scenery made things harder, since now she had everything she had always struggled for—and yet she still felt that emptiness inside of her. Her dissatisfaction led her to develop a guilt of sorts: she was someone who seemingly had it all and who was "indulging" in her own unhappiness. At least partially.

Ariela's family was Jewish and, even though she wasn't a practicing one, she observed the traditions and had a rich spiritual life. According to her daughters, she always told them she had a direct line to God. For that reason, she reactivated her spiritual connection and with this she began a deep process of inner search and self-knowledge.

One day, and in an act of sheer impertinence, she asked Andrés, a coworker with whom she practically had no relationship, but who always seemed at peace with himself, the following question:

—"How do you manage to stay always happy?"

She didn't know if it was truly happiness, but Andrés irradiated an inner peace that was enviable. It seemed as if he were fully aware of what he was doing with his life. It turned out that this workmate was an "explorer of consciousness", something that he kept in absolute secrete.

They quickly became friends. He opened a path for her to consciousness, spirituality and life's meaning. That knowledge became fundamental for her. She was glimpsing at a world that was previously unknown to her. One that was much more profound and authentic. What left the deepest impression on her was an extremely simple phrase told to her by him, and which became the starting point for her own process:

—"You're looking to take responsibility for your own life. And that has a name. **It's called purpose.**"

Pure Authenticity

As we have seen so far, we frequently start this self-knowledge process by first getting to know that which we are *not*, as in the case of Ariela. Then comes the stage of finding out that which we truly are, our most authentic identity.

Authenticity is a value related to those who tell the truth, accept responsibility for their feelings and behaviors, and are honest and coherent with themselves and others. It's a kind of honesty with yourself that takes place when actions stem from our most intimate being, and not because of patterns that have been imposed or assimilated through our contexts and that don't belong to us truly. It is the kind of action that we recognize as truly our own, the ones that allow us to palpate our limits, our potential and weaknesses. It is also expressed as a fidelity to yourself in both spirit and character. And they don't take deceptions.

What's authentic is always deep, thoughtful and intense. It can be an authentic pleasure, an authentic feeling or an authentic misfortune. That's why it awakens and intensely summons those feelings that are more properly ours. It is precisely that intensity that we must look for, since once we feel it we can recognize what's important for us, that which moves us and invites us to live intensely.

Authenticity is a condition that people must have and cultivate if they wish to improve. It's like an interior transparency that harmonizes and gives unity to our origin, destiny, biography and freedom. It is a virtue, a habit acquired through repetition. And therefore, those who aren't authentic can turn that around. And those who are can lose that quality if they aren't careful enough[75].

Aristotle claims that authentic people are reliable, since they always act in the same way, no matter who's in front of them. In other words, they're predictable as far as their moral integrity goes. They are as open with those who share their opinions as they are with those who don't. Authenticity has morals that are vitalist in that it wants and affirms life, trying to intensify it. It's not about saying the first thing that comes to mind, or a destructive comment. It's much deeper than that, as can be appreciated in the following story.

Palliative nurse practitioner Bronnie Ware, who worked her whole life with terminally ill people, wrote a book describing the five most usual regrets she saw in her patients before they died[76]. The most frequent was: "I wish I had had the courage to live according to my authentic identity, and not other people's expectations of me."

We will say this over and over again throughout this book, as if it were a mantra: **living with purpose requires the deepest level of coherence between who you are and your place in the world.** It's understanding what's beneath all the norms, dogmas and social beliefs we have acquired in life, which hinder our encounter with ourselves. Only that way we'll know what it is to be truly happy. For that, we must not fear pain.

Like Peeling an Onion

Self-knowledge is a difficult process. The deeper we get, the greater the need to cry may be. That's why it's like peeling an onion. In the outer layer we have our actions, emotions and thoughts. In the middle, our values, and that way until we reach the center: what we truly are. As we approach our identity, the harder it gets but the deeper the transformation will be.

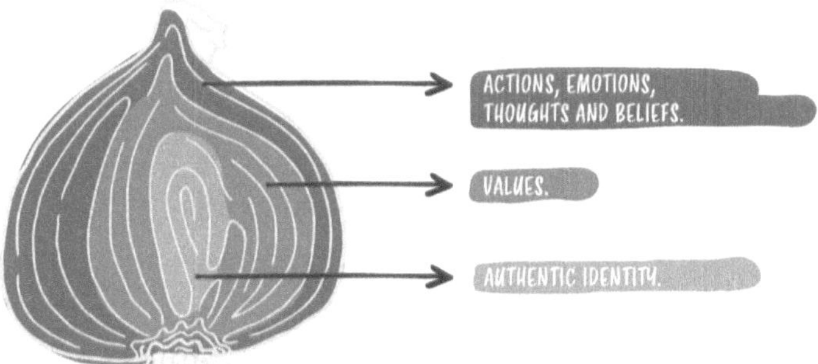

The problem with peeling the onion is that we don't like doing it, in the same way that we don't enjoy observing ourselves. If we're mad, jealous or act motivated by revenge, we're usually the last to notice.

The only way to know ourselves and observe our actions, emotions and thoughts, is to question ourselves constantly. Question the cause for our jealousy or anger, and analyze the situation with perspective through our consciousness

How did Ariela do it?

Let's go back to her story:

Now that Ariela knew that her void would disappear once she started her path to purpose, she was able to start her journey of self-knowledge. The first themes that came to her mind were: trying to distinguish what her passions were, what ideals moved her, what things about her life made sense, which had been propelled by her and which by others.

This new way of facing life brought her hopes, and she started seeing each day as an opportunity to learn something new and find experiences that would unleash the love she felt for her partner and her daughters, which she now wanted to share with the whole world.

Throughout this process, Ariela had to face some things that had caused her a lot of pain, like the fact that she never liked tennis and that she was afraid of saying so because she didn't want her parents to reject her. Other similar events were her forced return to Chile, and having been forced into a conflict of loyalties between her husband and her parents. While becoming aware of these episodes and the pain they caused her was hard, it was also extremely liberating.

What was liberating was realizing that these episodes didn't affect her feelings for her parents. She still loved them deeply and was grateful for all the love she felt from them. She found out that the mistakes made by our loved ones and the pain they can cause us don't cancel the love and affection we feel for them. By becoming aware of this, we leave our suffering behind and manage to preserve the deep connection that cements our bond with those family members that for whatever reason hurt us. This lesson marked Ariela very deeply.

Once she was free from her pain and the expectations of others, she was able to see herself without the filters provided by properness. It was then that her true values reappeared: the young college woman with opinions of her own, curious, who dreamed of changing the world. This strong and feisty woman who had vanished from the earth all those years of being a tennis player, a daughter, a wife, a mother and a lawyer. Those were nice roles and secured her the acceptance of those around her—but they didn't reflect who she really was.

Ariela understood that there's no other way but surrendering to our own vulnerability, so that we can be seen by letting authenticity be the protagonist instead of the character we have built for ourselves. While we let go of the control stemming from these beliefs, a feeling of inner freedom and peace emerges. One that we had been repressing involuntarily[77].

In this journey of self-discovery, she began therapy, or something closer to coaching. She also started meditating, and developed a very fine sensitivity, which allowed her to enjoy life with a different intensity. Good things became better—but also, mankind's pains started feeling like her own.

Something inside of her began to stir. Her longings, goals, the things that she would feel passionate about, lost the sense of priority they once had. Other priorities, more spiritual, came up. A new path opened up for her, one that promised to be one way. You could say that her process of self-knowledge took her to unsuspected places. She was astonished by this. How could an inner transformation, she wondered, be so deep without the exterior having changed at all?

Ariela found her true identity and started her path to purpose. She worked as a consultant for foundations, promoted volunteer work, and created social programs. She put all her knowledge as a lawyer in the service of the community. To achieve that, she was lucky her vision coincided with that of the leaders of her company. She met her most creative and efficient side, and discovered an overflowing inner strength which made her feel more alive than ever.

Her enthusiasm was such that for a second she thought it could drive her away from Alberto and the girls, the things she loved the most. But it was the opposite: her love and energy multiplied by a thousand. It wasn't about abandoning what she was, but of attaching meaning to it. She was no longer seeking her own happiness, but feeling part of something bigger. She now had found her place. She was contributing.

And then all of those synchronic encounters took place. She was no longer alone, hundreds like her were searching for the same thing and had an infinite desire to contribute, and a lot of love to give.

Her true identity took hold, so much so that Ariela decided to pause her career as a lawyer. She kept working as a consultant for companies and foundations but this time she did it hand in hand with corporate sustainability. That is to say, she was helping companies have a positive impact in their social, economic, environmental and human development environment. When she told her closed ones about this change of direction, they had a hard time understanding why she was abandoning everything she had built with so much sacrifice— and venturing into something they couldn't even figure out what it was. The most frequent question she was asked was, "What is that sustainability thing?" but this time Ariela did't care what others could say.

***

As some of you might've guessed, Ariela's story is, actually, my own. Now that I know myself better, I know I'm not comfortable telling it in the first person, which is why I found this alterative way of sharing it with you. Without a doubt, it's the story that I know best, and no other character could supply the sincerity I wanted to imprint when discussing the importance of knowing our most authentic identity.

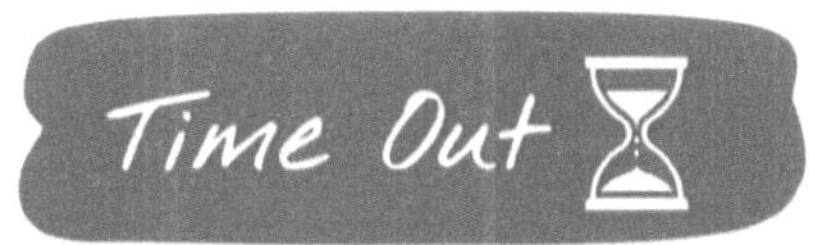

Write your "P objective": _______________________________

____

____

Answer the following questions:

1. Do you feel like this objective reflects who you truly are?

2. Are you aware of the requirements and implications associated with this objective, for you and others?

3. How important is it for you that this objective leads you to be accepted by others?

Second Element:
Passion

Making a Living Doing What You Love

Eduardo Della Maggiora is what I would call a passionate person. When we were teenagers, we would play tennis at Estadio Israelita and, besides being an excellent hitting partner, I was always surprised by how much he enjoyed it. He would spend whole afternoons on the court. It was clear that he liked tennis and that he would've become a professional player if he had had the necessary skills.

While he didn't become a tennis player, his excellent performance at school opened the doors for him to study Civil Engineering in one of the best schools in the country. And immediately afterwards, he started working for a prestigious bank in New York. In a few years, he became the Chilean referent at Wall Street. But to everyone's surprise, instead of choosing to keep ascending in his "successful" career, at the early age of thirty-two he quit and went searching for his purpose.

First, he went and lived for six months in Africa, where he met first hand the cruel reality of child malnutrition. Carrying that pain, he returned to Chile to do what he really loved: sports. But instead of going back to the courts, Eduardo used his talents to design one of the most brilliant social projects ever seen in recent times: Burn to Give (currently, Betterfly). Eduardo came up with a company which seeks to solve world hunger through sports. The business model consists of people registered in his app transforming the calories they lose by working out into food rations for minors with malnutrition. The rations are funded through donations or sponsorships from companies seeking advertisement, or through positive impact human resources programs.

Despite being a fairly recent project, they have already established themselves in forty-nine countries through their online platform, and, most importantly, they have already fed more than six thousand children and delivered almost six hundred thousand food rations[78].

Eduardo fulfilled a dream many of us have—making a living doing what we're passionate about. To achieve that, he used his greatest strengths: creativity and intelligence.

****

Ikigai and Something Else

To develop our passion, we will pick up the valuable lessons of the Japanese philosophy of ikagai (you can learn about it in detail in Appendix I). According to it, purpose of all human beings can be found in the intersection of four pillars: what we love to do, what we are good at, what we can get paid for, and our contribution to the world[79].

For the *telos* methodology we will use some of the elements of the *Ikigai* to describe the concept of passion. So, to get to know our passion and see how viable it is to make a living doing it, we must ask ourselves the following questions:

> *1. What do I love doing?*
> *2. What am I good at?*
> *3. Can I make a living doing it?*

1. What Do I Love Doing

We can tell we love doing something when we feel a strong inclination towards it. It's something we like, love and enjoy doing. It feels important, dear to us, and we are willing to invest a big portion of our time and energy doing it[80].

In general, that love moves towards an activity or a cause. If it's an activity, what we do becomes the most important thing; but if it's a cause, what we do becomes secondary, because we're motivated by the reasons behind what we do.

Love Towars and Activity

When this kind of love takes place, if it were up to us, we would spend all of our time doing it. That's how much we enjoy doing it. When this happens, it's hard to feel fulfilled unless we dedicate ourselves fully to this activity. Surely, Lionel Messi can't imagine a life without soccer, or Shakira one away from music, the same way Dante Alighieri couldn't live without poetry, or Michelangelo Buonarotti without art.

> Examples of activities:
> 1/ Sport activities: soccer, tennis, chess, climbing...
> 2/ Artistic activities: painting, dancing, writing, music composing, cooking...
> 3/ Intellectual or professional activities: astronomy, engineering, philosophy, research, technology, innovation, business ventures...
> 4/ Spiritual activities: mysticism, priesthood, contemplation...

Some people have a hard time feeling passionate about a single activity. We might have fascinating hobbies, but that hardly translates to exclusively dedicating our time to them, let alone our whole lives. We tend to confuse this type of passion with purpose, but in time we realize that purpose is a far wider concept, which involves much more than loving what we do.

Loving a Cause

On the other, we have loving a cause. In theory, we all have the potential of discovering a cause, struggle or ideal worth giving ourselves to. We're talking about causes that move us from the deepest, because they are likely determined or in accordance to our priority values.

> Examples of causes:
> 1/ Social causes: ending poverty, child obesity.
> 2/ Political causes: gender equality, rights of migrants.
> 3/ Religious causes: protection of the church, Christian values, religious proselytism.
> 4/ Cultural causes: promoting the arts, access to culture democratization, innovation.

Here, the things we do to make progress in a cause are of little importance. If I have to carry food boxes to bring them to the camps, or if I have to go to the protests on Fridays to raise awareness about human rights, it doesn't matter. What matters is why I do the things I do. As for me, I'm convinced it will be the companies that will contribute the most in the fight against inequality and climate change. That's why I work in the corporate sustainability area of a consulting firm. Doing or revising sustainability reports is far from being an exciting job. But I'm still passionate about it, simply because I deeply believe in the cause behind it.

Passion is generated, more than in the work itself, through valuing and visualizing our causes. Which is why the level of awareness about the direct impact our actions have makes all the difference.

It Feels Good

At the same time, passions give us pleasant feelings, nice and intense emotions. When we are experiencing one, the brain releases two neurochemicals, dopamine and oxytocin, which, as we saw before, are responsible for producing enough satisfaction and joy that we're motivated to keep trying[81]. We've all experienced that, probably. For instance, playing with our band, or our favorite sport, or cooking to please our guests—or defending a cause that we're deeply identified with.

Whatever we are passionate about will kindle our creativity[82] and make us highly efficient in that sphere[83]. As demonstrated by Adam Grant's studies, loving what you do stimulates motivation, perseverance, performance and productivity when it comes to achieve long term goals[84].

Being clear about the role that pleasure plays in the path to our happiness is fundamental, especially when we must choose where to invest the most precious thing we have: our time and energy. Instead of evaluating our goals based on what we can do and then see, out of our available options, which ones we enjoy, why not start the other way around? Let's see first what brings us joy and then evaluate our available options.

It's important to know that, when a new interest appears, it usually goes unnoticed. We might not even realize it's there. In order to discover and recognize it, we need to go through a long and proactive period of development, until we're finally convinced that it's something worth investing our time and energy.

The first time we try to play an instrument, practice a sport or a new trade, it doesn't come easy. On the contrary, it's difficult and sometimes we're discouraged by that difficulty. But it is precisely in those moments that we must persevere and understand that a reasonable amount of time is needed to evaluate if what we're getting to know is an interesting experience for us or not. The key is to dare.

Often, we begin an activity or project without great ambitions but in time they captivate us. Eventually, after a period of trial and error, most people start preferring certain activities over others, especially those which they enjoy doing. Out of these activities, a few will be perceived as particularly significant and will resonate in the way we see ourselves. When this happens, we might say that a special link has been formed between the person and the activity—and that we're seeing the first trace of how we wish to live our purpose.

Questions that might help you find out what you love:
- *What activities or causes do you feel energized by?*
- *What activities or causes would you fight for, even if you didn't get paid for it?*
- *If you could work anywhere, doing what you wanted, what would that be?*

Is It Really Important to Me?

We can say that we're in front of a passion when we find an activity or cause that we care about and which brings us such satisfaction that we're willing to choose it over every other option—in fact, give other options away so that we can concentrate our time and energy in it. For that reason, if we have to make an effort we will as if it were a good thing. As André Gide once said, "the secret of happiness is not doing what one likes, but liking what one has to do". This means that we can postpone physical pleasure and still be happy.

This way of conceiving effort implies stepping away from the belief that it is synonymous with unhappiness—a conception widely spread in a hypermodern society which idolizes pleasure. In the East they have a different view on effort, one that as a culture we should perhaps try to imitate. They think of it as a positive thing: if it's good for the person, for their body and consciousness, then it must be something nice, even if at first some resistance must be overcome[85].

If a passion weren't important enough to influence our decisions or actions, or worth the effort, then it wouldn't be a passion but a hobby—which doesn't mean they can't switch places later on.

For instance, my sister-in-law loves cooking. If she has any spare time, she'll spend it trying different recipes and preparing new dishes. She enjoys it, undoubtedly, as it relaxes her and distracts her from her problems. And she's very good at it. But when I ask her why she doesn't commit to it fully, she's adamant: she wouldn't leave her career as a psychologist. Also, she can't picture herself cooking all day. It's only fun as a complementary activity, a mere hobby.

On the contrary, Minsu Bang, a renown Japanese chef living in Chile, is entirely devoted to his passion. From the day he opened his first restaurant, Ichiban, every decision he makes, everything he says or does, is related to the art of the kitchen. He worries about every detail, getting the best products, training the waiters to be the best, greeting each of his customers to see if they're enjoying their experience, and constantly studying the world's new trends to be ahead at all times. He's fully committed, mind and body, with his passion, which brings him a great satisfaction.

Family and Social Capital

The things that we feel passionate about are frequently and to a certain degree determined by our family, schooling and our immediate surroundings. And while we might not be fully aware of these influences, experience shows that our roots influence our preferences and, consequently, our passions. This happens because our knowledge of those activities depends to a great deal of what we have been shown since we were little. As Aristotle says, "the road of discovery begins with the things that are familiar to us, and from then on we travel towards those we find harder to understand."

By watching our parents, we have a greater knowledge of their professions, which might spark an interest in us. In the same way, having been born into a religious family can facilitate the path to a spiritual life. Or being part of an ethnic minority can make us want to fight for equality.

If one of the trades, activities or causes that we have been around during our childhood and youth seems interesting, we will likely delve into it until it becomes our passion. On the contrary, if we weren't interested in any of them, we won't pursue them. One way or another, we can't deny that our family capital influences us, positive or negatively. It's important to reflect about this sphere in order to discover our true passion in a conscious way.

2. What I am I Good At?

We all have many interests that capture our attention and enthusiasm. However, considering our path to purpose, we will refer to those passions that will be prominent in our lives, and for which we must have the necessary capacities to perform adequately. The level of demand will depend on what we wish to achieve, and also from the level of competition in the market.

Strengths

Strengths are those positive qualities, which are admired and respected socially[86], and which generally evolve, through effort and dedication, from a natural born talent to a strength.

These are capacities that we already have within but which we must cultivate to develop our full potential. Practicing them contributes to our well-being, improves our relationships and allows us to contribute better to society. They also give us energy, which in turn makes us feel happy, well-balanced and wanting more.

We can find out more about who we are by knowing our strengths and finding out the qualities that can help us become admirable people by fully developing them. Some might grow with such force that will outshine the rest, but that doesn't mean they're not there.

According to the authors behind Strengths Quest, "in a way, the development and application of our strengths to an activity generates the notion that we're fulfilling our purpose. This exciting and satisfying process should bring a life of great satisfaction and joy"[87].

The VIA Institute on Character has classified strengths into twenty-four types, which can originate in the heart (when emotions, intuitions and relationships come into play), the mind (analytical, logical, focused on thought) or both:

Creativity	Perspective	Enthusiasm	Collaboration	Humility	Gratitude
Curiosity	Courage	Appreciation	Fairness	Precaution	Optimism
Judgment	Perseverance	Compassion	Leadership	Self-control	Humor
Love of Learning	Honesty	Social Intelligence	Forgiveness	Appreciation of Beauty	Spirituality

You can take the Via Survey strength test offered by the VIA Institute on Character for free at: www.viacharacter.org

Rodrigo's Strength

Rodrigo, a coworker, wanted to know his strengths, since in his opinion he wasn't so sure what they were. In this process he found out his greatest strength was his good judgement. At first, he didn't find it very attractive, because he associated it, wrongly, to a discrete and uncreative attitude. But upon reflection, he realized that having good judgment was a great quality, since it has allowed him to take wise decisions, even when the pressure is high.

Throughout his whole life, Rodrigo regretted not being bold enough and holding back when new opportunities arose. But once he discovered that his judgement was one of his characteristic strengths, he understood that it was an asset and used it to his advantage. His is observant, analytical, objective, has a great handling of his emotions and is open minded, all common characteristics in level-headed people. He's currently working a senior management position as a meddler for a multinational company. His capacity to anticipate conflicts and solve them in a friendly manner has brought him great returns.

> **Questions that can help you discover your strengths:**
> - *What jobs do you think you're good at?*
> - *Which ones come easily to you or seem to require less effort from you than from others?*
> - *Throughout your career, what projects or tasks have you excelled at?*

Talents

Strengths are enhanced when we use our talents, and we can perfect those with knowledge and constant work[88]. For that reason, and as we anticipated, while talents aren't the same as strengths, in many opportunities they are their triggering cause, and they can certainly facilitate the way to acquiring them.

It's important to have this in mind, since we tend to believe that we're only good at the things that we're extremely talented at, or that we must seek that for which we have a special gift or "superpower" that no one else has. This might prove helpful when our passion is also an activity, but it's not entirely true. Talent is only the beginning, and you need knowledge, practice and consistency to make the best out of it.

The belief that a talent is like a great divine gift has a religious origin that considers that talent a "calling" through which we serve God by using it. While talents are part of who we are, of our essence, we will see throughout this book that the path to purpose is much more complex than that.

Regarding talent, writer and psychologist Angela Duckworth has stated that it's problematic, because it makes us think that our success depends on it, shifting the focus from what's really important—our passion and perseverance, what she calls *grit*.

Duckworth believes that talent, in itself, is just the speed with which we get better at something. Thus, she claims that this is just an improvement rate associated with a natural advantage. In the end, the result will always be tied to an effort. What she's saying, in other words, is that talent is less important than we think for our success.

Maybe, in order to become the best tennis player in the world, or the most recognized painter of our times, a lot of talent is needed, since the speed with which we improve will make us take the lead. But being the best at something isn't the goal for most mortals—we settle for being good enough. What matters is the way in which we give ourselves to that which we want to accomplish. As Duckworth says, you can have all the talent in the world, but without the proper motivation to persevere and try hard, your natural advantage will no longer be relevant.

Developing her concept, Duckworth considers, as Darwin did, that motivation and effort are even more important than intellectual abilities: talent plus effort equals strength, and strength plus effort becomes a milestone, which is why effort is twice as important in the path to success.

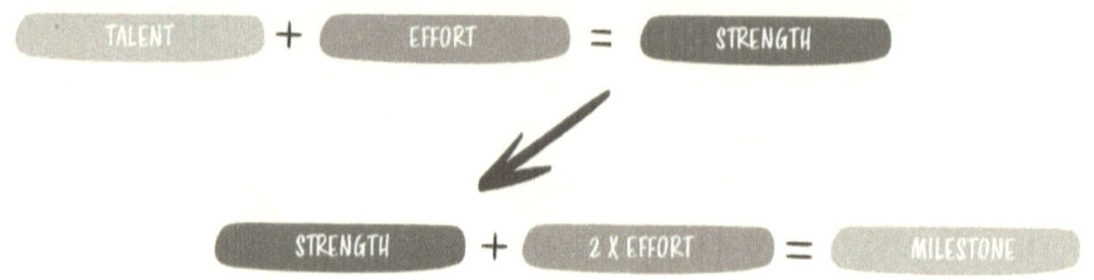

Flow

When we are doing that which we are passionate about, that is to say, what we love doing and where we apply our strengths, while also being challenged in a proper way, we experience an exquisite feeling, which psychologist Mihály Csíkszentmihályi has called flow. Csíkszentmihályi defines it as "a state in which people are so involved in an activity that nothing else seems to matter; the experience is so enjoyable that people will continue to do it even at great cost, for the sheer sake of doing it"[89].

Flow emerges when that which we love doing imposes an interesting challenge, for which we have the level of strength necessary to overcome and grow. That means that to reach that state we must realistically regard the challenge we're undertaking and our capacities. Otherwise, we would be talking about a dream or a mere aspiration. If the challenge's difficulty is greater than our capacities, we feel anxiety or even panic. Instead, if it's inferior to them, we get bored and feel like we're wasting our time. It's about finding a middle ground, as shown in the illustration:

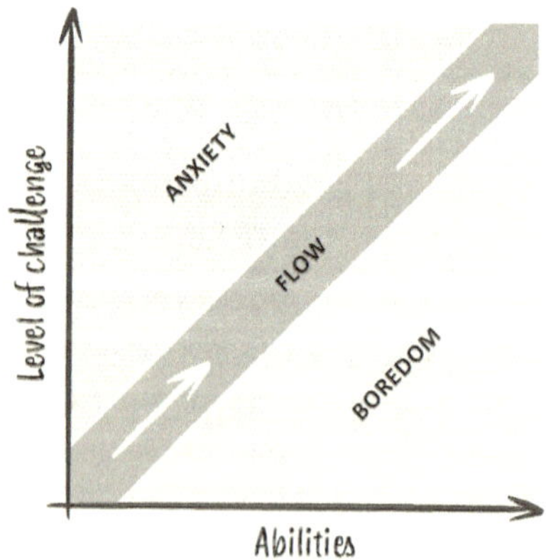

This graphic represents a determined activity for a particular person.

When we reach that middle ground, we will enter a state that will generate pleasure, enjoyment and creativity. It will be as if we were one with that activity, to the point of forgetting everything else, even the notion of ourselves and the passing of time. That's what an artist feels when they grab their paintbrush, a musician playing their instrument, an athlete playing a game. It's what I should've felt playing tennis but never did.

When María Sharápova, best tennis player in the WTA for several years and my training partner for a while, set out to be number one, her strengths and sports talents allowed her to be realistic regarding her possibilities while also having a career filled with moments of *flow*. My situation was entirely different: I was living a dream, a world of illusions and not reality, which prevented me from reaching that state of *flow* in tennis.

Personally, I lived through states of *flow* as an adult. In fact, writing this book has probably been one of the most powerful *flow* experiences of my life. I've put my whole heart and brain into it, and I have enjoyed every moment of the process. That fact alone makes it "worth the joy"[90] of having written it. I've been able to confirm to what extent *flow* can lead us to enjoy the present time, the process through which we put our full attention on the activity itself, letting go of the end result, which in this case would be accompanying people in their transformation towards a fuller life.

Purpose and Passion Are Not the Same Thing

Some people talk about passion as if it were synonymous with purpose. This happens when terms like calling, spark or vocation are used. They refer to passion as the only element of purpose, which it isn't. However, it might be the hardest to find (an activity that we love doing, a cause that we're willing to fight for) and thus they become interesting for the general public.

Passion alludes to our emotions, while purpose also includes the cause behind them. As Angela Duckworth says, whereas passionate people show higher levels of purpose, it's not a requisite. There are also passionate villains.

Simon Sinek's *Golden Circle* is a great tool for explaining this. He talks of the "why" and "how" and "what" of the things we do. In this scheme, passion[91] affects the "why" and the "what," but it doesn't consider the "how." In the path to purpose, unlike passion alone, the way we do things, the "how," takes a special importance, as you'll realize by reading this book.

That's why the path to purpose is a more complex and complete concept than passion, since it affects our "why," "how" and "what."

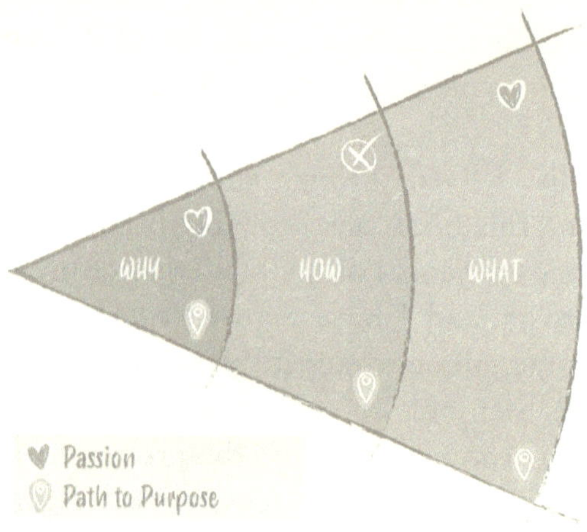

3. Can I Make a Living Doing This?

Going back to *ikigai*, and considering those "P objectives" centered around the sphere of work, financial sustainability (in other words, getting paid to do something) might keep our feet on the ground. Especially those of us willing to let go of everything to make the world a better place. Unfortunately, in the sphere of work it's not enough with loving what we do, or even being good at it—it must also be enough to maintain our livelihood. And while this might sound obvious, when our motivation is strong, we sometimes overlook that fact, as my friends Ignacio and Tomás can attest.

Ignacio and Tomás are great friends, but also share a deep conviction: they want to contribute with their work to making a better world. To fulfill their dream, they created their own organization: Fundación Interpreta [Interpret Foundation], which has carried out different innovative projects pursuing non-discrimination, whether for reasons of race, gender or religion[92].

Their projects generated a great social impact, but because they lacked a business model that made them sustainable, they didn't have the expected continuity. They earned public funds and they got sponsorships from companies, which helped them for a couple of years, but the projects weren't feasible in the long term. However, their convictions were so deep that, instead of closing their Foundation (which usually happens when there's no financing) they decided to divide it in order to stay united. Tomás stayed in charge of administering the Foundation, while Ignacio started a social intelligence consulting company, something closer to his area of expertise. They finance their life expenses with the consulting company, which allows us them to keep generating a positive impact through their Foundation.

Money, as a way of sustaining our lives, is as important as the other elements. While this is the least inspiring aspect of Japanese philosophy, it is without a doubt the most realistic one. We have to be practical... We can't live on air! If we don't know for sure how will pay our expenses by the end of the month, all of our attention and energy will turn to that and we will disregard our path to purpose.

I'm not saying you shouldn't follow your dreams—quite the opposite, you should! But you should also carefully plan them first. It's important to consider the timing. And instead of impulsively jumping into the pool, it would be wise to start gradually. Some people begin by working on their projects at night, after their formal jobs. Once these have taken shape, and their creators know to a certain degree that they can make a living by working on them, only then, they go ahead.

Here, the best advise is to think creative and flexibly, so that we can reinvent ourselves, see new opportunities and generate a sustainable model from our objectives.

I'm sure some of us wanted to become soccer players or singers when we were kids—but playing in the school team and singing at every school event is one thing, and it's quite another to make a living doing those things. As far as soccer goes, if we like it very much and we're very good at an amateur level, we must also evaluate if these conditions are enough to make it in a professional team. Otherwise, we won't be able to make a living and it wouldn't be right to have professionalism as an objective. It sounds harsh and conclusive, but unless it helps us pay our living expenses, we risk turning it into a nightmare instead of a way of achieving purpose. As Maslow rightly said, if our physiological needs aren't fully covered, our motivation will only seek to satisfy those, ignoring any other higher-level need from the pyramid.

This is what Aristotle meant when he discussed self-sufficiency, or *autarkeia*, which refers to people who are financially independent and don't require financial support from anyone. It's about a moral independence, says the philosopher, since having an adequate income allows us the freedom that we need in order to worry about achieving our happiness. And therefore, it is a responsibility for those who wish to live a good life.

If you love something and have the necessary strengths, but you can't get paid for it, then that shouldn't be your main activity. Of course, you can keep doing it, but you shouldn't dedicate most of your time to it. I know many people who, like me, started their path through volunteering. When we realized that our calling was deep, we decided to take a risk and transform a secondary activity into our main one. This can be the mid-range plan.

As it was discussed before, in purpose's philosophy of life, money can't be an end in itself, but a means for what we want to achieve. However, it we fail to consider the financial feasibility of our project and living expenses, money will become its main hurdle and therefore an end in itself, which is precisely what we want to avoid. By planning this we can avoid this contradiction.

* * *

The order in which we follow our passion is very important. If we start with something financially feasible or following our strengths, we might be restricting our options of enjoying what we're doing. As Ben-Shahar says, in order to find our passion, it's wise to start by doing what we love and then placing everything else around that, since working in something we're passionate about will not only improve our efficiency but also our happiness.

* * *

In relation to your "P objective," answer the following questions:

1. Do you feel as if the following characteristics apply to you?

   a) It's pleasant (makes you feel nice emotions).

   b) It stimulates you (awakens your creativity).

   c) You're good at it (you can apply your strengths).

   d) Makes you lose track of time.

2. How much of a priority is this objective?

3. How much effort are you willing to put forth to make it happen?

4. You do have a short or mid-range plan you can dedicate yourself to?

5. How far are you willing to risk your income for your objective?

Some recommendations for your self-knowledge process[93]:

1. *Pay attention to your beliefs:* allow yourself to observe your own thoughts, feelings and actions. Analyze your interpretation for each area of your life and put it into question—don't believe everything your mind shows you. Become a researcher of the history you tell yourself today and transform it into one that's more coherent with your true self—one that makes room to let go of control and allows for a new way of relating to yourself to appear, one that considers your dreams and your own capacity to make them real.

2. *Connect with your dreams*: ask yourself—what would you do if you had all the money and all the time in the world? How would you like the planet to look like in a hundred years? What fills you up with emotion and at the same time makes you lose track of time?

3. *Acknowledge your fears:* reflect about the worst thing that could happen if you go after your childhood dreams. If you didn't have that fear, what would you do?

4. *Take a step forward:* Rome wasn't built in a day. Empires start with a single brick. Talk to yourself. What step can you take today, how can you commit to moving forward with that dream? Move forward despite fear, courageously, towards your own authenticity.

5. **Establish boundaries:** delve into the challenges that might appear, and reflect resolutely on the boundaries you wish to put in your way. Those boundaries should divert you from everything that takes you away from who you are and who you want to become.

My Place In The World
Meaning Of Life And Transcendence

Purpose takes place in the doing. That is to say, when we actively situate ourselves in the world. In that interaction where we seek a coherence between who we are and what we do, as well as contributing to something bigger than ourselves. This way, "P objectives" and the goals we set should make sense to us and take us to transcendence.

> *A man without a goal is like a ship without a rudder".*
> Thomas Carlyle.

> *[When we live a purposeful life] we begin to steer a safe and steady course through the ups and downs of life, rather than being tossed about by them".*
> Rudof Steiner.

Third Element:
The Meaning of Life

> **"***The mystery of human existence lies not in just staying alive, but in finding something to live for"*.
> Fyodor Dostoyevsky.

Questions about the meaning of life date back to Ancient Greece. What's the origin and nature of life? What's its meaning or value? Who are we? Why are we here? All these queries have been addressed by philosophy, theology, psychology and the sciences, but there's no clear consensus as to what gives meaning to our lives.

Considering these questions, you'll appreciate a likeness between meaning and purpose. In fact, most authors discuss both concepts as if they were synonyms[94]. But while they are similar, reducing them in this way implies losing their individual inner richness. That's why, having in mind the *telos* methodology, we'll think of them as complementary concepts, but in a genus-species relationship—we have situated meaning as an element of purpose, that is to say, living with purpose gives meaning to our lives. We also have to keep in mind that other theories consider purpose an element of meaning and not the other way around as I have suggested.

Thus, the meaning of life is an element of purpose for the following reasons:

1. It cognitively unifies our intention with "P. objectives."
2. It lets us create a tale about our place in the world.
3. It allows us to perceive our lives as meaningful or important.

Let's look at each of them in detail.

In Time, It Unifies Intentions with "P objectives"

As human beings, we have the ability to ascribe meaning to whatever happens in our life trajectory. This allows us to unify different experiences, abstracting ourselves from what's concrete about each of them. Through this exercise, we can intellectually unite our intentions with the objectives we set for ourselves. If "P objectives" don't make sense to us, that's simply because they're not consistent with who we are.

The exercise of uniting our intentions to our objectives is something we do all the time, from the simpler aspects of our daily life to the more complex ones. That which doesn't make sense to us, seems absurd and we avoid it.

Luke has always believed in family as a legally constituted institution—but getting married was never in his radar, since gay marriage isn't an option in his country. Two years into dating Jerome, the opportunity to live abroad presented itself. They migrated to a more modern country, with a more egalitarian legislation. They didn't hesitate and got married. It was important to them to swear before the State that they would be faithful for life—even if they knew that their oath wouldn't be recognized as such when they returned to their country.

Anthony and Mark's story is different. They've been together for over twenty years, they live under the same roof, and they have two dogs and a cat that are like their children. There's romanticism, friendship and they share their patrimony through a society constituted to that end. For them, and for everyone else, their relationship is an engagement for life, even if there's no contract involved. Javier and Juan don't think that there's any value in a ceremony and rule out that they would ever need one to strengthen their bond.

The ability to ascribe meaning operates at a personal level—no one but yourself can know if something makes sense in your life or not. For some, marriage is meaningful, whereas for others it simply isn't. While this ability operates in an almost automatic fashion, we can delve into the meaning we ascribe to events if we have a higher level of consciousness. As human beings, we're machines that build meaning, but the quality and impact that that meaning has in each of us will be determined, mostly, by our capacity to observe and reflection upon it.

Throughout this process, we seek to establish connections between emotions, ideas, memories, events, people and objects that aren't physically related to each other[95]. This represents the most sophisticated level of interpreting information[96]. In the words of Michael F. Steger, "[m]eaning is the web of connections, understandings, and interpretations that help us comprehend our experience and formulate plans directing our energies to the achievement of our desired future"[97]. Only then we're able to perceive that which we are has a level of correspondence or coherence with what we do in the world.

Therefore, as Mihály Csíkszentmihályi points out, our life becomes meaningful when we're certain that the objectives we set for ourselves are connected around purpose, and that there's a temporal order and a causal relationship between them[98].

This characteristic of human beings couldn't be applied in all of its magnitude if it weren't for our capacity for hope. The tale about our lives implies a unity in the time continuum, unifying our memories from the past with the present and future. And there's one thing that makes this time connection possible, that is to say, the link between our intention (past and present) and our objectives (future): hope.

Hope is our capacity to evolve in time, to be-in-time, which allows us to have or keep a direction and not succumb to the anguish provoked by the passing of time. Ricardo Capponi calls it "pleasure in waiting," because it allows us to enjoy the ride. It's the pleasant feeling that emerges when we know that something good, or that we long for, will come. For instance, knowing that one day my book will be published keeps me motivated during the writing process, even if I have no certainty as to when that time will come.

Building Our Own Tale

Each time we try to understand our life and place in the world, we tell a story about ourselves and our passage through time. There's a meaning that stems out of this tale, as Yuval Noah Harari says: "When we look or the meaning of life, we want a story that will explain what reality is all about and what my particular role is in the cosmic drama. This role makes me a part of something bigger than myself, and gives meaning to all my experiences and choices"[99].

Harari points out that, in actuality, all stories are incomplete, which doesn't prevent us from attaching meaning to them—we just need a role to fulfill that's bigger than our horizons. It doesn't have to ring true for everyone as long as it does for us. It could be mere fiction and still provide us with an identity and the feeling that our lives make sense. Without this cognitive process, life would simply be a series of isolated events that don't come together in a unified and coherent whole. We wouldn't be able to explain our passing through the world.

Feeling that Our Life Is Meaningful

A meaningful life makes us experience our life path as an important thing[100]. It tells us that we have a place in the world and that we do things that are meaningful to us and to those we care about. In other words, it prevents us from thinking that our lives don't matter—the things we do, no matter how small or simple, deserve our commitment and dedication[101].

Looking for meaning in our lives can occasionally bring pain to our souls; however, it always contributes to our path to purpose. It can generate pain, struggle, even anger—but once we get there, it's one of those things that we feel proud and fulfilled for having done them.

What are those objectives that seem so important that we're willing to risk it all? Or, as Mark Manson says, life is a constant loop of solving problems, and solving them makes it meaningful. We can't run away (it would mean we're in denial) or free ourselves from them, because as soon as we solve one our brain will find the way to invent another. But one thing we can do is choose problems whose solutions we care about, so that we don't get trapped in solving obstacles we don't give a damn about—that's how life becomes more meaningful.

The answer to the question about life's meaning is probably one of the most debated topics out there—and there is no consensus yet. However, fur purposes of the *telos*, when we talk about objectives that are important, we will be referring to sources of meaning.

Sources of Meaning

Each need that we seek to satisfy implies solving a problem, in a certain way. This search and resolution is the origin of meaning for our lives, and that's why it becomes a source of meaning.

Why do we have the needs or desires that we have? No one has ever given a satisfactory answer to this question. The only thing we know is that our needs and desires are somehow determined by our biology, history, and culture.

Irena Sendler was born on 15 February 1910 in Poland. Her father, Stanislaw, was a well-known physician in her hometown of Warsaw. With an admirable story of courage and purpose,

he passed away when Irena was only seven. Back then, the typhus epidemic threatened the lives of everyone in the city, and Stanislaw was one of the few who dared treat those we were sick, knowing full well the high risk of contagion involved. Many of the people he saved were Jewish.

When he died, as a gesture of retribution and gratitude, they offered to pay for Irena's education. The strong bond created from her childhood with the Jewish people in Poland led her to defend their equal rights, which were being denied all over Europe. Just before the start of World War II, Irena fervently opposed the discrimination system adopted by some universities and was suspended from Warsaw University for a long time.

Thus, and inspired by her father's innate abilities to take care and empathize with the helpless, she decided to go to nursing school. When Germany invaded Poland in 1939, Irena was working for the Social Well-being Department of Warsaw, which ran the soup kitchens in the city. Thousands of people went there every day in search of food, medicines, health care and shelter.

In 1940, the Nazis began confining Jews to specific neighborhoods, and created the Warsaw Ghetto. Irena, horrified by the living conditions there, joined Zegota (the Council to Aid Jews) and got a permit for entering the ghetto without restrictions. Once there, she made the necessary contacts to smuggle out as many children as possible.

Convincing their parents was extremely difficult—since they were staying inside, they had to assume they would never see them again. Irena couldn't promise that the children would stay alive, which made it even harder. But there was one thing they all knew for certain: if the children stayed inside they would die. Irena was a ray of hope. She managed to save over two thousand Jewish children, risking her own life.

Irena had to face big concerns to save each one of those kids. However, she chose to tackle those concerns, which shows just how powerful meaning in our lives can be when it comes to making decisions. So much so that we're willing to make huge personal sacrifices after a greater good. The meaning of life is perhaps the least rewarding element of purpose, since it doesn't necessarily imply any emotional joy. It presupposes such a generosity that we might risk our own life looking to contribute to a cause or collective destiny that exceeds by far our strict personal coordinates.

Decades later, when she was asked during an interview why she did what she did, she answered: "The reason can be found in my home, in my childhood. I was brought up to believe that a person must be rescued when drowning, regardless of religion or nationality"[102].

Irena was recognized by the State of Israel as Righteous Among the Nations, the highest recognition given to those who helped the Jewish people during the Holocaust. Besides, she was awarded Poland's highest civil honor, the Order of the White Eagle.

* * *

In Irena's case, saving the life of Jewish children triggered in her the need to contribute to a bigger cause. But there are endless needs that can also give meaning to our lives. In more realistic or quotidian scenarios (less heroic for sure), if for instance we're afraid of being fired from our jobs, we will have to satisfy and compensate for a bigger need for security if we don't want to fall pray to anguish. Our if our partner has left us for someone else, our self-esteem will take a big blow that will likely have us trying to alleviate this lack.

With this in mind, let's review the different ways of classifying these needs or sources of meaning, using Maslow's pyramid[103]:

1. Security	Every person needs to have a degree of certainty and stability. We connect this with basic securities, of a rather material nature, like having a roof above our heads that no one can take away, a job that pays enough to make a living, available health care when needed, or knowing we can go out without suffering aggressions.
2. Belonging	Human beings are social creatures. Because of our biology, we need to bond, connect, cooperate and reproduce with other people, increasing thus our chances of survival as a species. The desire to connect with others is as important in our lives as finding food or pleasure[104]. **The need to be a part of something, whether it is forming a family, building intimate relationships, friendships or workgroups, is the most recurring source of meaning. About this there's consensus in the literature.**

3. Self-esteem	The need for self-esteem or self-respect forces us to constantly evaluate ourselves. It invites us to feel and know the value of our own lives. It's the need to feel comfortable by being authentic and putting our capacities into practice. Throughout this process, we also seek to feel validated in front of others, to feel proud, admired and respected by those around us. The true measure of someone's self-esteem isn't determined by their positive experiences but rather by how they manage the negative ones[105]. Having the right self-esteem is necessary to functioning properly as a human being[106].
4. Self-realization	Self-realization is the answer to one of the most elevated needs of the human being: developing their potential to the max. Trying to be the best version of themselves or everything they can aspire to be. Our evolution as a species encourages to seek our own growth. We need to be constantly developing ourselves physical, emotional, intellectual and spiritually. This drives us to stand out, be the best, dominate an art, permanently make progress or deepen our knowledge. It means challenging ourselves continuously, and it requires a certain cleverness, practice, suspense, adapting to changes, and high levels of curiosity. It also demands courage to get out of our comfort zone and venture into the growth zone.
5. Transcendence	To transcend is to go beyond, that is to say, out of the limits imposed by the physical or material plane, the one perceivable by the senses. That's why it requires the existence of something bigger than us. We can transcend in many different ways, for instance when we love someone, or create something new or different, when we inspire others or serve them. About this central issue of purpose we will talk in detail next.

"P objectives" that we set for ourselves can satisfy more than one need simultaneously. For instance:

Eva has always lived in the same place and is very comfortable there, but a good friend of hers has invited her to partake in his startup, in which there are other young people who are as passionate as she is about the environment and who are looking for technological solutions to promote a circular economy.

- Sources of meaning: belonging and transcendence.

Henry wants to get a promotion. He's been building his career as an academic in a single university, hoping that he'll get a management position that will allow him to implement new learning techniques for philosophy students. He knows he has the necessary abilities and can turn the career around.

- Sources of meaning: self-esteem and self-realization.

It might sound obvious, but not every need or problem can give meaning to our lives. They must be important needs which take a period of time to be satisfied. Finding the prettiest dress for the party, choosing a restaurant to have lunch with my friends— while these choices satisfy immediate needs, they don't give the kind of meaning that we're looking for here.

At the same time, not everything we do will generate that kind of meaning. In truth, as we mature the things that we really care about are frequently reduced, and so our choices will get more and more relevant to ourselves. Without realizing it, as we opt for those things that make sense to us, we define our values and who we are deep down.

Exercise: Peak Experiences

Peak experiences are those situations in which we feel an intense joy, peace and well-being, and our lives present themselves as meaningful, even if for a short time. We've all had those kinds of moments in life. They're events that should easily appear when we remember our past, because by shaking our emotions they become engraved in memory.

I would like to invite you all to do this exercise of discovery. It will take a few hours and you should be, as far as possible, in a state of calm and inner peace, ideally somewhere where you are in direct contact with nature. When this happens, start remembering those experiences, situations, events or moments that evoke a feeling of happiness for one, some or all of the following reasons:

1/ You remember them with pride.

2/ You feel grateful that they took place.

3/ You feel those experiences or situations were completely authentic.

4/ You would repeat those experiences, given the circumstances (even if this is hypothetical, considering that our age is probably not the same as when they took place).

5/ They are, in general, simple experiences that seemingly have no greater meaning or relevance to a third person, but which for some reason have shaped your life. This mark makes them special only to you.

I did this exercise some years ago, and it took me a couple of months to relive those moments that had been most meaningful to me (much longer than a few hours). It was a progressive process, as if one memory brought me to the next, and so on, until I was able to develop them chronologically. I was surprised to realize that there were several shared patterns between them. If I looked at them with perspective, they said a lot about who I was and my values.

Without a doubt, this exercise has helped me know myself better, and understand which are the things that I care about enough to cope with negative emotions for them.

To better illustrate their significance, I want to share my peak experiences exercise, an itinerary that was key to better know who I was, and to build my own path to purpose in the sphere that has been the most difficult for me: work. I hope it will be as useful for you as it was for me.

Peak Experiences that Opened my Eyes to what Was Really Important:

Thanksgiving

This experience happened when I was a teenager. As I mentioned before, when I was fifteen I lived in a tennis academy located in Tampa, Florida. There were young people there from all over the world, who dreamed of becoming professional tennis players. It was November, Thanksgiving, the most important holiday in American culture, when families gather and give thanks for the good things in life along with a hearty meal.

My family wasn't there and it wasn't a holiday that I felt as my own. I hadn't been in the States long enough to assimilate, but I still accepted Mrs. Becky's invitation with enthusiasm. She was my English teacher at the time and she invited me to a soup kitchen. I didn't have a clue of what that was, or what we were supposed to do there, but my reaction was automatic, as was that of three other academy volunteers (yes, very few of us signed up for it).

We got to that area's soup kitchen, which was impeccable—the tables had nice tablecloths and actual china, not the plastic kind—and saw a huge counter full of hearty food that looked delicious (volunteers were not supposed to try the food). We were told that we had to get in line to set the trays and then take them to the tables so that everyone felt well cared for.

Contrary to what I expected, hunger was not the problem. I got the impression that no one was there for the food but rather for companionship, to take someone to talk to. So I disobeyed the orders they gave us and followed my gut.

I felt that if I stayed there with Mrs. Becky and the other volunteers, just watching, that experience would be meaningless. I sensed those people's loneliness. And I understood them, for I felt alone too. So I sat down with each of them and one by one they told me their stories and asked about mine. I realized that for them, somehow, keeping them company and listening to them was much more important than the food. I felt useful and authentic at the same time... a feeling I wasn't used to, but one that I liked.

Each one of those dialogues was in itself extraordinary and enriching. To my surprise, I understood that I had much more in common with those people that I would've ever imagined. For once, we shared the same pain, being away from our families, and precisely during a holiday that is a loud reminder of how important that circle is.

A week after that episode, I received a letter from a history teacher I had had the previous semester. In the envelope there was also a clip from the local newspaper Tampa Bay Tribune, dated November 24th of the year 2000, which had a picture of me helping in the soup kitchen during Thanksgiving. The teacher letter read: "Sharoni, there's an immense world out there—follow your instincts, you have a lot to give. Seeing you like this has made me immensely happy."

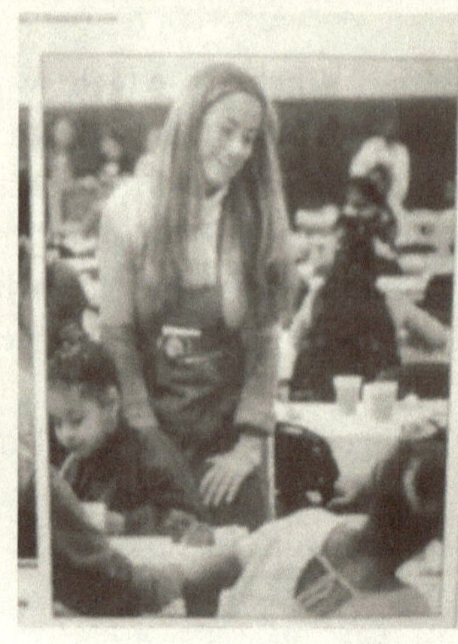

Photograph:
Local newspaper clipping.

Over the years, I've come to realize that that experience helped me connect somehow with the universal aspect of what's human. It was also the first time I took a proactive stance, and that connected me to an inner energy I didn't know I had. I felt like myself, authentically, free from the minute I chose to follow my instinct instead of the script. Also for the first time I perceived the sort of gratification that comes from contributing, even if for a few hours, to other people's well-being. And I discovered a strength that until then I didn't know I had: an ability to empathize and connect with others.

Fundación Techo [Roof Foundation]

When I was eighteen, I went back to Chile and enrolled in college. One day, as my first year in law school was coming to an end, a friend invited me to a meeting of the Un Techo Para Chile [A Roof for Chile] foundation (today, just Techo), where they asked our help with their campaign to raise money for winter works.

This campaign consisted in giving little bags with charcoal inside to those who donated money on the street. I thought it was an absurd idea, a meaningless effort. But it was the first time I was in touch with a foundation, and I was looking for ways of permanently contributing, instead of having a single Saturday night experience. Then I had the opportunity to overhear a conversation between two coordinators about the shanty towns eradication model they were putting into practice. "What's that?", I thought. They explained what a shanty town was (land occupied illegally, with very precarious housing, overcrowded families, without access to basic services). People who lived under those conditions were eligible, with the help of the foundation, for state subsidies to get their own definitive home.

This part about eradication made a lot more sense to me. We all have the right to a home and to live without fearing that someone might kick us out at any moment. It was an important issue and I became instantly interested in getting involved.

I began collaborating with the Fundación Techo in a project that aimed to eradicate the Sagrada Family shanty town, located in the neighborhood of Renca. It consisted of relocating the sixty families that lived there in a subsidized housing neighborhood. After a thorough search, we were able to buy the neighboring land thanks to state subsidies, and the long-awaited construction of social housing took place. It took five years of hard work, which at that age feels like an eternity, but it was by far the most satisfactory result of any job I've ever done. An experience that makes me proud to this day and that gave me the first clues about my path to purpose: contributing to the well-being of others made me feel complete.

It is as curious as it is gratifying to note that in recent years I have met again many of the same young people who worked for Fundación Techo back then. It seems that foundations that promote youth volunteering sow in many of us a seed of purpose that makes us sooner or later go back to it. I emphasize this, since I firmly believe that volunteering should not only be evaluated in relation to the material results they get to their direct beneficiaries, but also as effective mechanisms for the development of the cultural and social capital of young volunteers.

This experience taught me endless things about myself: that the biggest satisfactions in life require an equal amount of effort; that abandoning your certainties allows for a type of learning that's fundamental to personal growth; that I could achieve anything I put my heart to; that important solutions require solutions that come from the community; and, above all, that human richness is infinite, and that there is no socioeconomic, religious, or generational gap that can divide us when we have a common purpose.

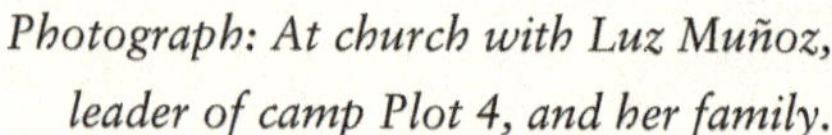

Photograph: At church with Luz Muñoz,
leader of camp Plot 4, and her family.

Professional Internship

Shortly after, I had another peak experience. As many of you know, in order to get your law degree in Chile, after having completed all your courses, you have to do a free six-month professional internship for the state. Many would complain about this and even considered it an expropriatory requirement. But for me it was the gift of "experience" and "experiences."

I did my internship at Corporación de Asistencia Judicial [Legal Aid Corporation], specifically at the Quilicura headquarters in Santiago. Their mission is to help vulnerable people have access to justice. During those six months, I had to process civil and labor lawsuits. I oversaw more than a hundred lawsuits, which was enough work to keep me entertained five days a week. Besides, I liked getting to court at 8 a.m., since I knew that officials would pay more attention then and the lawsuits could be sped up. I closed more than half of those lawsuits, many through conciliation settlements, reaching agreements that generated income to both my clients and the corporation.

I was in my element. I felt that I was a useful lawyer, my profession made sense because I could help many that without this service could've never settled their conflicts in court. This internship was particularly helpful for realizing that through my profession I could help improve other people's lives. This time I learned that my contribution will always have a bigger impact from a place of specific knowledge instead of mere volunteering. Without a doubt, it made more sense to work as a lawyer than do something else I wasn't knowledgeable at.

An ambition also arose in me that was unknown to me until then: I was eager to reach agreements, finding solutions, speed up cases and raise as much money as I could for my clients. I wanted to be my better version. An eagerness I never had in tennis had emerged in court with the strength of a hurricane.

When this experience ended, I felt the world crumbling down on me. For two months, I cried every morning, thinking that after this came "work life" and that I would never feel the same again.

Taxes

There were two courses that I really liked in law school: labor law and tax law. Our tax law professor motivated us a lot, which is not common for that career. Eduardo helped us look beyond the laws themselves, showing us how tax policies can affect the dynamics of society. For instance, tax collection policies can correct social behaviors. That's the case with the tax on alcohol or tobacco, which aims not only to collect money but also to discourage consumption. He also made us realize that some taxes can redistribute wealth, as it happens with income tax, while others are less fair, like value-added tax, which has a fixed rate for all taxpayers regardless of their income and is used worldwide because of its efficient collection. In short, he made us aware of how important tax policy is when it comes to citizens contributing to the collective well-being.

I was captivated by tax law because of that professor. Since then, I was seduced by the idea of becoming a tax law attorney. I was lucky enough to get hired by one of the most important consulting firms in that field—PricewaterhouseCoopers, now called "PwC."

What was I doing when I did this exercise?
I had been working as a lawyer for ten years. And while studying taxes and its professional practice had made sense at first, over the years this interest started winding down. As I had anticipated, I realized that tax consulting for big corporations was far from my desire to relate to the social world. I was being true to the value of justice, but when I asked myself "Justice for whom?", what I did didn't feel important anymore. Not because big corporations didn't need defending (then can also fall victim to injustice) but because hundreds of lawyers were doing the same thing. If it wasn't me, someone else would do it. I didn't feel any ambition for growth, and I wasn't projecting myself forward. Unlike many of my coworkers, I never felt that desire to become a partner. And that's when it started losing all of its meaning.

Although I didn't want to continue with taxes, I really liked that company, and felt a knot in my stomach each time I thought I had to leave a place that had become a second home for me. I was in a conflict, but luckily the partners understood my change of heart. With great generosity, they encouraged me to promote an area of social responsibility that was in the making. We started offering foundations, SMEs and vulnerable people pro-bono legal services.

Then we led a project called "Chileincluye" [Chileincludes], supporting migrants and in particular Syrian refugees who came to Chile, in partnership with the government and the UN. It benefited over ten thousand people. This was a particularly touching work for me. I had to struggle against prejudice for being a "Jew" seeking support for "Arabs." At first my authentic intention was put into question, and even the government believed at one point that I was Mossad (Israeli intelligence). But this didn't stop me. Shortly after, and with the communication that such a situation warranted, all conspiracy theories were discarded, and it ended up being a high social impact project, which made a lot of sense for me. During this process I met great people, Arabs too, which I consider dear friends to this day. This experience struck me deeply, and I found the true potential of purpose.

Then, more and new projects came up, and as they started acquiring more and more importance, we decided to enter a new stage. That way, after a short while, a new dream came true: the partners supported me in constituting the Fundación PwC Chile [PwC Chile Foundation].

Ever since then, I began feeling a different kind of gratification, one that comes from choosing the problems I want to face, which makes me feel like a free and fully happy woman.

* * *

Finally, if each of us freely decides what needs he seeks or thinks are important to satisfy, these needs will contribute to our path to purpose as long as they let us transcend[107], as we will see with the next element of *telos*.

Considering your "P objective," answer the following questions:

1. Do you feel like this objective belongs to the path of life that you have drawn for yourself?

2. Do you have any hope to achieve it?

3. By setting an objective and trying to achieve it, you seek to satisfy certain needs. Do you know which they are?

   a) I'm looking to feel safe.

   b) I'm looking for a sense of belonging.

   c) It makes me value myself more.

   d) I'm looking to reach my full potential.

   e) I'm looking to contribute to something bigger than myself (other people, society, nature, etc.)

   f) I'm not sure.

4. Do you feel that this objective is consistent with who you are?

Fourth Element:
Transcendence

As long as there is poverty in this world, no man can be totally rich even if he has a billion dollars".
Martin Luther King Jr.

Aung San Suu Kyi: The Heroine of Democracy

Aung San Suu Kyi was born in Burma (now, Myanmar) in 1945. She is the daughter of Aung San, a Burmese national hero who achieved his country's independence from the British Empire in 1947 and founded the Burma's modern army. Much loved and respected by the people, he was assassinated short after, supposedly by political rivals who opposed independence. Her mother, Khin Kyi, was also relevant in Burma's history. In 1960 she was appointed ambassador to India and Nepal, and Suu Kyi joined her and left her country behind.

She went to England for college, and studied philosophy, politics and economics. After finishing her studies, she worked at the UN New York headquarters. During this time, she met Michael Aris, a British academic who specializes in Tibetan culture. When she was twenty-six years old they got married and had two children.

Afterwards, Suu Kyi took care of their children, their home and also helped her husband with his academic work. She spent sixteen happy years living in England, with a beautiful family and happily married, until she received a phone call in 1988 that would change her life forever: her mother was in poor health. She decided to return to her country after her long exile.

"The Lady," as she is called in her country, took the first available flight and went to Burma to see her ailing mother. Getting off the plane she found a devastated, oppressed and extremely poor country, with no room for public debate or the exercise of civil rights. Until then she had never been involved with politics, but she was overwhelmed by a deep feeling: a sort of responsibility towards her people. She decided to stay. This decision had the makings of a drama, because despite her family's support, she had to leave them behind, in England.

Inspired by Gandhi's no violence politics, Suu Kyi organized peaceful rallies all over the country, demanding authorities to hold free elections after twenty-six years of authoritarian rule, political repression and economic decline. Suu Kyi, transformed into a symbol of her country's democracy, suffered herself from the Burman military junta's repression, remaining deprived of her freedom for almost twenty years, most of them under house arrest. Despite having the option to return to England, she never reunited with her family, since the threat that the military wouldn't let her in when she returned to her native country was very real.

Those were extremely difficult years for her. Her husband and children were never given a visa and in ten years she was only able to see them on five different occasions. Most in their situation would've given up. But they didn't. Michael Aris was a brilliant man who stood by his wife. While she was arrested, he worked tenaciously behind the scenes to ensure her freedom and security. He used his knowledge, connections and everything within reach to give visibility to her cause and prevent her assassination. He even brought the case to the White House, the UN, the Vatican and the Norwegian committee for the Nobel Peace Prize.

In the late nineties, Michael was diagnosed with cancer. After finding out how serious his condition was, and knowing she wouldn't be able to physically say goodbye to him, Suu made a tape talking about their wonderful time together, their children and her unwavering love for him. Michael died two days before the tape arrived, in 1999.

From then onwards, Suu Kyi fought even harder, not only for her father's legacy, but also for the memory of the man who always stood by her and died fighting for her and her cause.

Although Suu Kyi has two "P objectives" in her path to purpose(her family and her commitment to the community), her desire to restore peace and democracy to her country, or her need of transcendence, were so important to her that she had to sacrifice her family.

Damages to her personal life, suffering, an uncertainty about her own fate, a feeling of injustice... nothing was able to stop something that she embraced as a collective and personal cause at the same time. Suu Kyi found a way to transcend through this objective, and this made her strong enough to overcome all misfortunes.

After over two decades of continuous house arrest, Suu Kyi reached her "P objective." The military had to give ground and elections were called, in which her party won by a wide margin. "The Lady" began working for the government, and became a world-renowned political leader. In 1991 she received the Nobel Peace Prize, and she will always be remembered as one of the world leaders in the struggle for democracy, freedom and peaceful resistance in front of oppression.

The year 2021 marks her personal history again, as the military took back the power through a coup.

Let's see now the last but most important element of purpose: transcendence.

* * *

What's transcendence?

Suu Kyi story of transcendence makes us wonder about that abandonment, about the need to get out of oneself to become part of something bigger—which is difficult to explain. The concept presents a range of different definitions, depending on the discipline through which we study it.

Originally, it aims to a phenomenon whose causes are outside oneself. In 1969, Abraham Maslow described thirty-five different ways of conceptualizing it, among which we find the following:

- The loss of self-consciousness
- Accepting the natural world
- Manifesting our dependency to others
- Being above the "us" and "them" polarity.
- Going beyond time and space.
- Experiencing the cosmic consciousness.

In terms of our developing of the *telos*, we will understand transcendence as:

> Contributing to something bigger than ourselves.

Looking to transcend implies the need to reach for something beyond our personal interests, something outside the limits imposed by the body, the physical, material or perceptible plane imposed by our senses. It's an attribute that alludes to what's immortal, essential and mystical—in other words, something that's difficult to apprehend for us because of those characteristics.

That "bigger something" is often of a spiritual or divine nature. Many achieve transcendence through their faith in God, while others can through other ways of spirituality. You can't become fulfilled or complete as a person before understanding your place in the higher order of things[108].

Conversations between Frankl and Maslow

If we had the privilege to witness a conversation between Viktor Frankl and Abraham Maslow on transcendence, the dialogue would probably go like this:

—Maslow: human being's fulfillment comes from their self-realization, from seeking to fully develop their potential.

—Frankl: Self-realization is without a doubt important, because it helps us grow. But have you ever wondered if there's something else? I've been observing the human being for decades. At a certain point of their existence, they need to address something or someone other than themselves.

—Maslow: Are you suggesting that true happiness comes from procuring it for others?

—Frankl: I am, at least partially. Purpose of life represents the desire to work towards our own well-being, but not only from a place of personal interest—also assuming an active commitment to others, whether it's family, community, the country or mankind. That's the path to true happiness.

—Maslow: Why do you think that is?

—Frankl: The more we forget about ourselves, giving ourselves up to a cause or a person, we become more human and as such we perfect ourselves[109].

A Few Years Later...

—Maslow: Dear Viktor, I've been thinking about our last conversation. I've been watching my patients to see if the things you claim are true. It would seem that there comes a point in the path to self-realization where we can only keep growing if we think, feel and act in a transcending way. By studying the cases of patients and public figures that have achieved a self-realization, that have managed to succeed professionally and have money and power, I was surprised to learn that only some of them consider themselves fully happy. Only those who have put their strengths and talents to the service of others.

—Frankl: I'm glad you were able to see it for yourself. Taking the path of transcendence means venturing into the better part of ourselves, one that's self-realized and connected to others. Self-realization means a life with others, and transcendence puts our own needs aside to serve something bigger: community, nature, the universe.

—Maslow: Indeed, you're right. And I must admit that it's been a sad spectacle to watch people that despite "having it all," remain unhappy[110].

—Frankl: The way I see it, we must strive for that virtuous circle in which the more I advance towards my self-realization, the bigger my possibilities of contributing to society are. And the more I transcend, the more I self-realize, and therefore the bigger my contribution to society can be, and so on.

The Circle of Transcendence

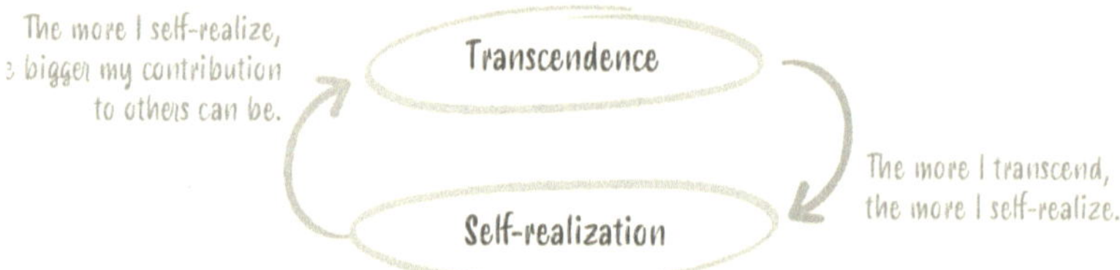

Maslow, greatly influenced by Viktor Frankl, redressed the top of his known pyramid of human needs. If at first self-realization was at the top, the final design adds a higher level—transcendence. In his last work, Maslow states that man belongs to an evolved species, and therefore possesses a superior transcending nature which is part of its essence[111].

Ever since then, Maslow considers transcendence the most elevated of human needs, the final degree of motivation. It's the highest level, the most inclusive and holistic of human consciousness[112]. And we'll only be able to reach the maximum realization of our potentials, or self-realization, once we put those capacities at the service of others.

This has been confirmed by different later studies, which indicate that individuals with transcending goals, beyond themselves, display more integrated personalities, a better adaptability and the willingness to achieve goals, greater openness to the world and levels of satisfaction in life, compared to individuals that only look out for their own interest. This has been reinforced by Angela Duckworth's Grit, a book where she points out that the people with the most grit are also the ones who seek to transcend the most[113].

The existence of a virtuous circle also finds its most rational explanation in our own human biology, as it was mentioned when we discussed the hormones that produce happiness. We have hormones that encourage us to seek our individual well-being and others, the collective. One might think that they are incompatible but on the contrary, the challenge lies in balancing them out.

Psychologist and strategic coach Cloe Madanes[114] provides a more practical perspective, by pointing out that by focusing on others, you will get better results for you as well, since:

> 1/ different contexts and experiences allow you to connect to others.
>
> 2/ by being needed by others, you feel your life is important.
>
> 3/ a spiritual link with the universe is created, which allows you to grow and create wonderful things.
>
> 4/ you feel grateful for being able to contribute.

Transcendence Demands that We Run Two Marathons

Imagine if we had to run two marathons: the first one means to satisfy your own needs, until you become self-realized. But once you're there, the only way to keep growing is to put our abilities to the service of others. Then the second marathon begins, consisting of holding other human being's hands (even if it's just one) and accompany as they progress in their own life marathon. It is within this second marathon that purpose's virtuous circle is achieved. In order to be better, to grow and to achieve happiness, I need and must carry other people with me to the top of the pyramid.

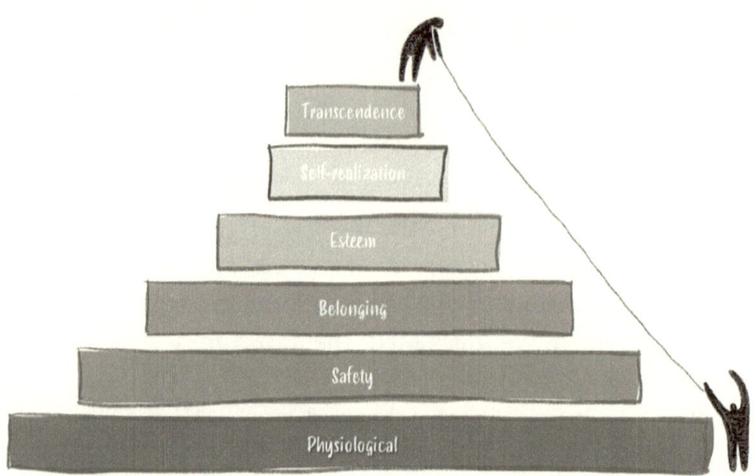

Transcendence Feeds on Virtue

In one of purpose workshops I do, I ask participants to observe themselves for a few days and write down the moments where they felt the happiest. Answers usually revolve around these topics: when they help a friend solve a problem, when they share an intimate moment with a love one, when they overcome a difficulty or limitation, when they create something new or innovative, when they are thankful for their lives or love.

These situations reflect on actions that make us feel good about ourselves and the world around us. This happens when each of them stems from a virtue and represents the right way of doing things. For that reason, in the language of the Golden Circle, virtues respond to how we do things. In the aforementioned examples we can observe how certain situations increase our level of well-being because they contain virtues such as service, truth, justice, friendship, courage, creativity, gratitude or love.

It's hard to understand why that is, but virtues posses all the necessary qualities to love them in themselves because they're good per se. Greeks called virtue areté, which in the XXI century is translated as "the psychological process that allows us to consistently think and act in ways that are as beneficial to us as they are to others"[115].

For instance, someone who seeks to achieve justice benefits themselves when they achieve it, but also society—because, by that act, society becomes more just. On the contrary, someone who acts looking to exert power over others, because of ambition or trying to satisfy their own shortcomings, wouldn't be able to transcend through their acts. In the path to purpose, objectives and goals must always be virtuous. In other words, they must always seek to do good, to themselves and others.

Our virtues shape our feelings and thoughts, determine our actions and allow us to realize ourselves[116]. Virtues are also ways of being, strong beliefs that seem essential to us. We make decisions and act according to what's important to us.

In *Nicomachean Ethics*, Aristotle states that the highest human good is "an activity of the soul in accordance to virtue."

Values and virtues usually resemble each other, but there's a genus-species relationship between them. The first represent what's important in life for people, and as such influence our path to purpose[117]—but they're not necessarily good for others and they don't necessarily prepare us to reach *Eudaimonia*, which is dependent on the context. Having power can be good if I use it to impart justice, but it can also be bad if I abuse those who are weaker. Because of this, there are bad and good values, and only the later can be virtuous.

Examples of Values[118]	*Examples of Virtues*
Power Social status, prestige, influence on others or resources.	**Altruism** Behaving in the best interest of others, selflessly.
Achievements Personal success by demonstrating competence according to social standards.	**Modesty** The quality of not being proud based on being aware of your own weaknesses.
Security Harmony and stability in society, our relationships and personally.	**Empathy** The ability to understand other people's feelings and emotions, based on acknowledging others as equals.

Respect Restricting actions or impulses that might affect or harm others, or that go against social norms.	**Tolerance** Acknowledging differences by respecting others and believing that no one owns the truth nor is completely right.
Traditions Acceptance and commitment to the roots and customs of our culture or religion.	**Courage** Having the courage to act even when we don't control the outcome.
Hedonism Pleasant life, with sensorial gratifications.	**Loyalty** A person's ability to remain faithful to a person, figure or symbol.
Transcendence or Universalism Understanding, appreciating, tolerating and protecting the well-being of all people and nature.	**Good Sense** Ability to rightly deliberate about what's good or bad in everyday life.
Self-determination Independence of thought and action. Being able to choose, create and explore.	**Justice** The ability to live in truth with others.
Family Caring about the well-being of our close ones.	**Love** Wanting someone's good.
Benevolence Understanding, appreciating and protecting the well-being of all human beings and the planet.	**Resilience** Capacity to overcome adverse circumstances.

How Can I Tell if my Actions Will Transcend?

One way of checking that your "P objective" contributes to something bigger, is to inquire into the value that underlies the action itself. If the values are virtuous, you'll transcend with your "P objective"—because virtue per se seeks the well-being of others. But if it's a purely instrumental value, which doesn't imply a virtue, more inquiring will be need, into intention.

For instance, if the value that moves me into doing something is power, I would have to wonder if I intent to manipulate or inspire people with that power. Or, if I'm looking for financial security, am I thinking of my own well-being or protecting my family as well?

We can classify them thus:

Individualistic Values:

1/ They're selfish and only seek our own benefit, even at the expense of others.

2/ They're superficial, concerned about finding material goods or things that imply superiority over others.

3/ They're beyond our control, depend on external factors; for example, buying a new car depends on having enough money, or being promoted depends on my superior's decision.

While they can be pleasant in the short term, they don't bring us closer to happiness. They don't bring us closer to our purpose.

Examples of Individualistic Values

- Being worshipped by others.
- Possessing many material things.
- Working on something economically profitable.
- Believing one's always right.
- Denying those problems one doesn't want to deal with.
- Taking revenge to teach others about their mistakes.
- Living as if good things will come later.

Transcendent Values:

1/ They seek benefit outside of themselves.

2/ They're based on reality, deal with the world as it is, not as we would like it to be.

3/ They can be controlled. That is to say, they depend on us and can be applied from the minute.

They can be reached internally through adopting a virtue, and lead us to our purpose.

Examples of Transcendent Values

- Showing affection to those one loves.
- Seeking a more aware or spiritual life.
- Generating a positive impact through one's work.
- Listening to those who care about us.
- Taking responsibility for one's problems.
- Inspiring others through our actions.
- Enjoying the present.

Are There Ignoble Purposes?

This is a great question, because the way we answer it will define whether purpose is a good thing or merely a concept based on a strong motivation which originates from an individual or collective passion. William Damon warned us that we should carefully distinguish a noble purpose (as synonymous of "P objective"), morally acceptable and admirable, from an ignoble or bad one, because they're clearly not the same thing[119].

There are several examples throughout history of people who satisfy their needs using destructive means. Someone getting rich through fraud, like Bernard Madoff in the United States or Alberto Chang in Chile, would be on the antipodes of purpose. Purpose invites us to contribute to society—only the right behavior will allow for our self-realization and transcendence.

Claiming that a purpose can be ignoble is the equivalent of stating that the end justifies the means. We all know Machiavelli's famous phrase, but purpose isn't any mean. It's the ultimate goal of human beings and therefore it can't be used as a synonym for any other. It is a much more complete concept. If the end is ignoble, we might be in the presence of a selfish objective or a passion, but never a purpose.

Examples from the World

Psychologist Jeremy Frimer carried out next to some colleagues an extensive analysis of influential figures from the past fifty years. They were looking at those who've been considered referents of a life of purpose[120]. The results showed that those people who were thought of as exemplary:

1/ Have humanistic principles and virtues, and showed a sustained commitment to their ideals.

2/ Are consistent in terms of actions and values.

3/ Are courageous, willing to sacrifice their own self-interest to stay faithful to their moral values.

4/ Inspire others and move the masses into acting according to moral standards.

5/ Are humble in relation to their own importance.

Considering these characteristics, the people that were chosen as exemplary were: Rosa Parks, Shirin Ebadi, Nelson Mandela, Mahatma Gandhi, Aung San Suu Kyi, Dalai Lama, Martin Luther King Jr., Andrei Sakharov, Emmeline Pankhurst and Eleonor Roosevelt.

The same study, and considering the same characteristics, also chose those influential figures that our history labels tyrants. Within that list there were names like Adolph Hitler's and Mao Tse-Tung's, people who even though met most of the criteria in terms of influence, were left out because there was no virtue in their lives. Instead of practicing transcendent values, their actions were motivated by power, money, status or controlling others.

It might be true that the previous characters, the exemplary ones as much as the tyrants, have histories marked by courage and leadership—but the big difference in their behavior is a moral one. Ultimately, the first group always acted on the interest of others[121]. Through their actions, they contributed to improving other people's lives.

Different Levels of Transcendence

While the word transcendence evokes a high emotional and spiritual state that's hard to reach, in a study conducted in 2009 a third of those interviewed claimed to have experienced this phenomenon[122].

Academic David Yaden[123], along with other college professors, has managed to determine the precise moment we go through these experiences, classifying them according to their level of fusion between the self and the world[124]. In short, we transcend when:

1/ We enter a state of flow.

2/ We meditate.

3/ We are astonished.

4/ We are inspired.

5/ We serve others, do altruistic things or fight for future generations.

6/ We feel gratitude towards something or someone.

7/ We live some sort of mystical experience.

8/ We experience love.

These states of consciousness are called "transcendent experiences." In them, our subjective meaning of ourselves as individuals can vanish temporarily, fused with others or our environment. This feeling implies the dissolution of the boundaries between our sense of self and the world, in order to achieve a union, like a unitary whole[125].

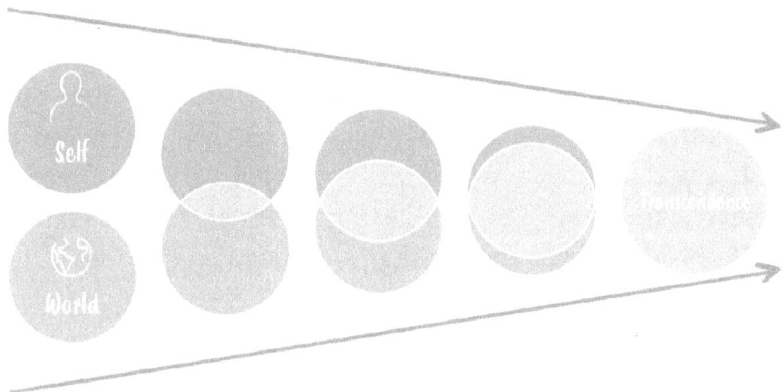

The bigger the fusion between the self and the world, the higher the level of transcendence.

These transitory states of consciousness are experience within an intensity spectrum that goes from the most routinary thing (for instance, entering a state of flow when we get lost in music or a book) to the most intense and potentially transformative (for instance, loving someone).

Transcendent states directly influence our physical and mental health, improve our family life, lessen our fear of death and encourage a sense of transcendence, because they increase our motivation to behave in a way that benefits others[126].

You can see a detailed description of different levels of transcendence in Appendix IV.

The Quantum Change

Intrigued by the highest or more mystical transcendent experiences, a couple of professors from the School of Psychology at New Mexico University began inquiring about a group of people who, at a certain point in their lives, experienced an extraordinary change[127]. Their patients described this change as "seeing the light." They published an ad in the local newspaper requesting volunteers who wished to share their story about an unexpected personal transformation. The barrage of responses was astonishing. Thus, they gathered hundreds of tales about epiphanies, sudden experiences and perceptions that they called "quantum change," through which they declared having accelerated their path to purpose.

They describe this change as a sudden "personal metamorphosis," which leads them to feel an experience as vivid, surprising, benevolent (in a way, a feeling of peace, serenity, happiness) and of a lasting personal transformation. It's about an intense change that is remembered in detail for life.

Something that's recurrent in many cases is the description of being immersed in something trivial when all of a sudden a voice is heard from the inside, making them view their life or the world in a completely different way.

A similar thing happened to my friend Gonzalo.

A couple of years ago I was lucky to meet him at a public tender. He's a commercial engineer and is less than forty years old. At the tender they were looking for innovative solutions to improve the migrant context in the country. His project consisted of an online platform called INMI, destined to help migrants and refugees find job opportunities[128].

I was part of the jury, and I witnessed Gonzalo's proposal (what self-starters call pitch). He was supposed to show us his project's attributes and convince us that it should be the winner. While a priori his platform wasn't quite innovative, since many similar apps already existed (even if not catered specifically for migrants), we were all left perplexed by his history.

He told us that one day he was looking out the window from his office, and something caught his eye. A long line of workers waiting to go into a construction site. The same thing happened the next day, and the line of people waiting kept getting longer. After a week of seeing this phenomenon repeated each day, Gonzalo decided to go look what was going on. A Haitian gentleman, trying to his best to speak Spanish, told him: "We're waiting for a worker to get injured so that one of us can take his place."

This episode marked a before and after in Gonzalo's life. Something that was hard to put into words wouldn't let him remain indifferent. It was as if an inner voice were directing him from that moment onwards. The next day he quit his job, his professional career, and all the comfort attached to them, and dedicated his life to solving a problem that was important to him and that resonated with his personal story and his values.

Gonzalo's project has been a reality from 2019. Until this book's publication, it has managed to connect over seven thousand people with a hundred companies throughout the country. It has also been awarded other tenders and exclusive contracts with the UN.

A similar thing happened to me a few years ago, while I was still working as a lawyer. I was in the middle of a typical business meeting with George, the owner of an important Chilean chain of restaurants, with whom I had a trusting relationship after having worked together for almost ten years. We used to have legal and tax planning meetings, where we would define corporate strategies, the defense of ongoing trials, and the allegations to Internal Revenue Service, among others.

César, my boss at the time and a great friend to this day, would be with me in these meetings. Because as a lawyer he was as brilliant as he was discreet, I was the one in charge of directing the meetings, knowing full well that César would come up with the best ideas. One of those days, I remember we were trying to go as fast as possible, since we all had other lunch commitments. No more than twenty minutes had passed since we began, when my hand dropped the pen it was holding and I stopped paying attention. My gaze was lost somewhere in the horizon, as if it needed a pause to observe my body coming out of a deep dark hole and rise above the mountain. I stopped listening to what was being said in the meeting. During those minutes, I felt I was being spoken in a language that doesn't exist and in slow motion. As if my language wires had been crossed. I was no longer making notes or asking questions, and César had to rescue me by taking control. The meeting went on and I was no longer there. Just my body.

Suddenly, and as if my whole career could be summed up in a few seconds, I discovered that the work that I was doing had little to do with who I wanted to be. With the impact I wanted to make in the world. With what was important to me: improving other people's lives.

We left the meeting and César, worried about me, took me by the arms and affectionately asked me, "What happened in there? We totally lost you".

César is like a brother to me, which is why I think we both knew what was happening to me. I could no longer postpone an urgent matter. The time had come to stop investing my time and energy in something that I was very comfortable doing, and instead venture into what I had wanted for so long—changing the world through purpose. That very same week we coordinated my transfer from PwC's legal area to the sustainability one.

I heard about this study for the first time in Wayne Dyer's movie *The Shift*, where he emphasizes that this kind of change makes people reevaluate their values. Transforming their priorities, putting first what's important. While the names "quantum change" or "mystical experience" might sound dark or mysterious, the stories collected in the study, similar to Gonzalo's or mine, are not about any of that, but rather about moments of profound authenticity.

The most relevant part of the study is that it shows how our values change after we experience transformations as the ones described. In the following table we can see how women and men described their main values (from a list of fifty choices) before and after their transformation experience.

Change in value priorities:

👤 (before)	👤 (after)	👤 (before)	👤 (after)
1. Family	1. Personal growth	1. Wealth	1. Spirituality
2. Independence	2. Self-esteem	2. Adventure	2. Individual peace
3. Career	3. Spirituality	3. Achievement	3. Family
4. Being socially accepted in diverse contexts.	4. Happiness	4. Pleasure	4. God's will
5. Physical attractiveness	5. Generosity	5. Being respected	5. Honesty

We haven't displayed the full list here, but the study reveals how virtuous or transcendent values, like spirituality or individual peace, went from the bottom to the top of priorities. On the other hand, values of an individualistic character (not necessarily virtuous), like material richness and physical attractiveness, went down. In general, both men and women showed a big increase in the value attached to forgiveness, generosity, God's will, personal growth, honesty, humility and love.

This leaves us with the conclusion that these experiences can wake us up, or accelerate our path to purpose, by opening our minds and preparing us for the self-realization and transcendence that we're looking.

The Balance of the Altruist

As we strive to reach our "P objectives," we must find a way to balance our interests with those of the others, and transcendence with our general well-being. If we don't, we might mistakenly generate a big impact but fail to contribute to our happiness.

In his book *Give and Take*, Adam Grant, expert on behavioral psychology, distinguishes three types of people considering their social interaction[129].

1/ Givers, always helping others even when the personal cost of doing it is bigger than the reward.

2/ Takers, who by being strategic in everything they do, only help others when the benefit for themselves is greater than the cost.

3/ Matchers, who under the principle of reciprocity, help others as long as they're helped in return.

In his studies, Grant has discovered that givers are dichotomic: they're either the most or the least successful people within a group. That is to say, in a pyramid of success they're both at the highest and at the lowest. Eager to understand that abysmal difference, Grant created a new category: abnegated givers. They are those who have an unhealth relationship with their surroundings, since their actions go against their own interests. To the point where, wanting to help others, they harm themselves.

In one of his research studies, Grant tried to find out why abnegated givers lowered their grades in college. By interviewing each of them separately, he realized that they had something in common—they all acknowledged having missed classes and hours of study because they were helping others solve their personal problems.

Grant concludes that successful givers are as ambitious as takers and matchers. But, unlike abnegated ones, they protect their own interests. His conclusions make one thing evident: caring about others and oneself aren't incompatible things. Givers get to the top precisely because of that combination.

In 2008, Bill Gates said it in a similar way at the World Economic Forum: "There are two great forces of human nature: self-interest and caring for others"[130]. This is the greatest human power. Caring about benefitting others, keeping ambitious goals that will allow us to advance in our self-realization and transcendence.

Psychologist David Bakan[131] has studies the duality through which we look after our own interest and that of others. He calls the first one agency, and the second communion. According to Bakan, agency implies self-protection and affirmation, whereas communion implies participation, contact, openness, unity and voluntary cooperation. For Bakan, an optimal mental health requires integrating both modes, having a combination between self-interest and caring for others. Modern studies have confirmed this hypothesis, and have associated integrating both modes with having positive results in social relationships, growth, integrity and general well-being[132].

Do you have a well-balanced life? Answer the following questions and find out:

- Do I have healthy boundaries? (Physical, Mental, Spiritual.)
- Do I worry about my own well-being? (For instance, meditating, eating healthy, doing exercise, spending time with family and friends, etc.) And about not hurting anyone?
- Do I have a good self-esteem and stop others from taking advantage of me?
- Do I balance my own needs with those of others?
- Despite giving a lot to others, do I know when I need to recharge my energy?
- Do I allow myself to have fun, even if it doesn't help others?
- Do I prioritize my own personal projects over other people's demands?
- Do I know how to say no?

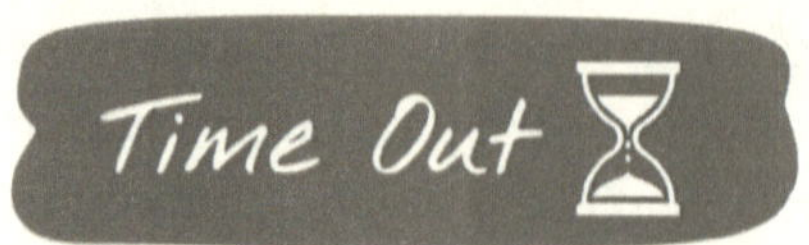

In relation to your "P objective," answer the following questions:

1. Do you believe this objective will help improve other people's lives?

2. How important is it to you that it helps improving other people's lives?

3. What do you hope to achieve by working towards your objective?

   a) Experience contexts and situations that will allow me to connect with others.

   b) Generate a spiritual link with the universe that lets me grow and create wonderful things.

   c) Feel grateful to be in a position to contribute.

   d) Be part of something bigger than myself.

4. Do you feel capable of achieving a balance between self-realization and transcendence?

The *Telos* Core

> **"***I am not what happened to me.
> I am what I choose to become***".**

Carl Jung.

So far we've managed to know the core of the *telos*, or of our path to purpose. We have reviewed in detail its four elements, which in turn we classified in two dimensions:

- **Who am I:** authenticity and passion.
- **My place in the world:** meaning of life and transcendence.

TELOS CORE

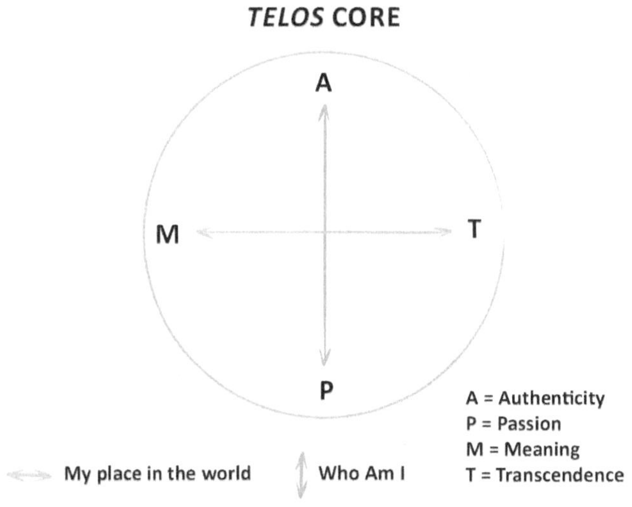

These four elements will contribute to our path to purpose as long as they reflect our intention in a faithful manner, and are also present in our "P objectives."

The Time has Come to Check Your Own Personal Map!

To verify that you have correctly designed your path to purpose, you must review the correct relationship between the four elements of the *telos* with your intention and each of your "P objectives":

	Intention	"P objectives"
Authenticity	My authentic intention is what motivates me.	My "P objectives" are an expression of who I am, consciously and connected with my emotions.
Passion	They are an expression of deep inclination towards an activity or cause that is really important to me.	My "P objectives" have been chosen considering what I love doing and my strengths. In the work sphere I have also considered that it be financially sustainable.
Meaning	I make sense of them from a cognitive perspective.	My "P objectives" must be consistent with my intention giving me hope, helping me build my own tale, and making me feel that what I'm doing matters.
Transcendence	My actions are motivated by my intention to contribute to something bigger than myself.	My "P objectives" are noble and virtuously contribute to my well-being as much as to other people's. The priorities in my values have changed to be more transcendent.

This review is no easy task because (and I won't get tired of saying this) **we are complex beings.** And trying to conceptually simplify our human nature is what leads us to make wrong decisions.

The level of depth of the *telos* methodology aims to determine which elements from the path to purpose are working well, and which aren't in our personal map (and not by trying to simplify what purpose really is, but rather by clearly delimitating its four elements). If you stop and examine each separately, it will be easier to appreciate if there's one that's not working as you would want it. This allows you to make better decisions and the necessary changes.

> To know the level in which your "P objectives" are contributing to your path to purpose, you can take the *telos* test on my website
> www.sharonirosenberg.com

The Transformation

When the four elements of the *telos* are present in life, we start experiencing a transformation in our values, priorities and interests. The values that were deeply ingrained start losing relevance, and what used to seem distant or useless suddenly becomes important and prized.

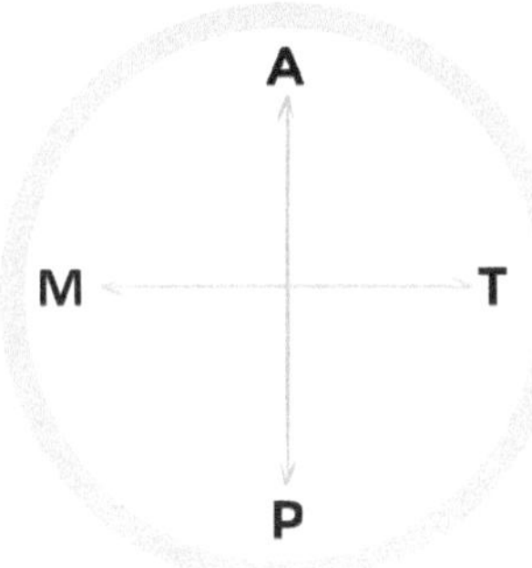

The transformation in our values is the first impact that a life of purpose has on us.

In order to change our individualistic values, which are not good to us, for transcendental ones which enhance our virtue, we must be able of question them. The path to purpose is an invitation for doing so. For observing them in all their shortcomings, consequences, impact they have on us and others, and prejudices associated with them. This is a hard process, because our identity feels threatened, which makes us want to avoid it. It's normal to try to protect our values, and justify them to others, because they are part of what we are. But purpose pushes us forward this transformation.

Our values determine the nature of our problems, and this will determine our quality of life. For that very simple reason, if we want to change our problems, we must change our values, and consequently the way in which we measure success and failure. That's where purpose plays a central role.

You could say purpose invites us to organize our life in a different way, around these new values, as if it were a philosophy or way of life. It's not about caring for other things, but rather the contrary, so that we can invest the most precious thing in our lives (our time and energy) in that which is truly relevant. Thus, without our realizing it, all the details that hinder our everyday life begin to dissipate.

PART III:
HOW THE PATH TO PURPOSE
IMPACTS YOUR LIFE

We've seen that purpose's first impact in our lives is the transformation of our values and priorities. Now we'll see the second impact, activating our intrinsic motivation, and the third, happiness.

Motivation, The Best Sign That You're On Your Way

Be the change you wish to see in the world".
Mahatma Gandhi.

The Rhesus macaque (Macaca mulatta) is a species of primate famous for having been the subject of experiments that made great scientific advances for humanity possible. For instance, the blood group Rh factor was named in its honor, because it was first identified in these monkeys. They were also sent into space by NASA in 1950, and are the first primates cloned: Tetra, born in 2000.

Although they're known for their multiple exploits, in this book we're interested in one that's derived from a research conducted by American psychologist Harry Harlow in the 1950s. For two weeks, Harlow studies eight Rhesus monkeys. The primates were locked in a room with various puzzles, which consisted of moving a lock, adjusting it with a hook and then returning it to its original position. The monkeys spontaneously began playing with this puzzle, focused and determined, apparently enjoying the activity. They solved the puzzle quickly, despite no one having taught them how or promised a reward for it.

Not ageing with animal testing, and considering that these weren't aggressive tests, the conclusions of the study were valuable for humanity. They showed that monkeys solved the puzzle simply because it felt rewarding to them. Since then, Harlow began building a theory of a third human impulse—complementary to the two already discovered, seeking pleasure and avoiding pain—which he called "motivation."

This third animal impulse was defined decades later[133], in relation to human beings, as "that innate and natural propension to commit to activities that we're interested in, exercising our own abilities in order to conquer optimal challenges"[134].

***

Why is it important to talk about motivation?
Because studies show[135] that when we're living our purpose, that is to say, when we are authentic, act with passion, our actions are charged with meaning, and we contribute to the well-being of others, our motivation increases in such a way that we are ready to achieve the goals we have set for oursel-ves. Motivation is the way we have to check that our personal map is working properly, and that our objectives are taking us towards our purpose.

By activation motivation, we are filled with an overflowing energy which allows us to overcome our limits and reach goals and objectives we didn't think were possible. I'm not talking about any kind of motivation, though, since there are two classifications:

1/ Intrinsic, when it's self-generated, as in this case.
2/ Extrinsic, when it's caused by elements beyond our control.

Let's see what they consist of, so that we can clearly identify which one directs us towards our objectives—because, in this path, we must activate intrinsic motivation.

Intrinsic Motivation

As we have already pointed out, human nature is designed to mobilize people towards achieving goals, ensuring that the actions they take *flow* without further obstruction on their part. When this goal is consistent with who we are, with our intention, there's a satisfaction that exists merely because it was voluntarily and freely forged in our minds. In addition to this, by being authentic and genuine, this motivation also generates positive emotions in us.

When motivation is activated by the mere satisfaction provoked in us by doing an activity, whether it challenges us, entertains us, or we feel that we're making a difference in the world—this motivation is understood as intrinsic.

People who activate this kind of intrinsic motivation or energy are the ones who usually live and enjoy challenges as part of a process, not looking for success nor eager to reach the goal line. They know they can come close to perfection, even awfully close, but that they will never get there. They find joy pursuing the goal rather than in getting there.

Certain authors state that intrinsic motivation is the authentic one, and that it should be awaken in people who wish to change or achieve real behavioral progress[136]. Being intrinsically motivated means taking on a challenge personally and creatively[137]. This happens with our goals in the path to purpose, which is why we seem to have an inexhaustible energy to achieve them.

From a more spiritual perspective, Eckhart Tolle[138] refers to intrinsic motivation as "enthusiasm," and describes it as a creative power that goes beyond what a single person can ordinarily do. Tolle points out that this enthusiasm originates from uniting that which we are passionate about with our purpose, which generates an immense energy and intensity, like an arrow on a direct path to a target, enjoying its ride.

Tolle thinks enthusiasm comes from our essence and, generally, overcomes all the hurdles and difficulties that we can find throughout our lives so that we can carry our purpose. A person guided by enthusiasm doesn't differentiate between winners and losers. In fact, they seek to include others. They don't use nor manipulate people, because they are a creative power themselves and therefore don't need to steal energy from a secondary source.

Extrinsic Motivation

There's a different kind of motivation, one that unlike the intrinsic one, comes from external elements. It aims to carry out an activity to get a specific result, different and independent from the activity in itself. A typical example would be performance bonuses or job promotions that companies set to motivate their workers into getting better results than the ones projected.

Fabrizzio and Roland, who studied Journalism together, dreamed of becoming sports journalists and commenting the Olympics, or the world tennis and soccer championships on television, of having their own show promoting young athletes, of travelling the world following major sports events. It shouldn't come as a surprise that achieving all of that is extremely hard, but Roland persevered in his dream and started working as an assistant on a TV network. He had a low salary, worked without a contract and from sunrise to sunset. On the other hand, Fabrizzio was tempted by the benefits of working for a bank, and chose a job as an account executive. By the end of each semester he received a performance bonus and after five years he got a promotion and became a manager. These were the incentives that kept him from quitting his job, since he definitely didn't enjoy it. Here, Roland chose a job motivated intrinsically, whereas Fabrizzio followed an extrinsic motivation.

It goes without saying that the motivation needed for a life of purpose should be intrinsic, at least for the most part, because often extrinsic motivations converge as well. In Roland's case, he must also consider that his job should pay for his living expenses.

A Superpower

Viktor Frankl argues that the purpose of life provides the basis for human motivation, which he called "noetic"[139]. I don't want to sound like a reductionist, but this began breaking the paradigm that man is only moved by pleasure, as Freud said, or power, as Adler claimed. Instead, he moves mainly by that which reunites him with his purpose and gives meaning to his life.

If we were to put into a graph what motivation generates in us when we live a life of purpose, it would be the engine allowing us to move forward from where we are right now (point A) to where I want to go, that is, total happiness (point B).

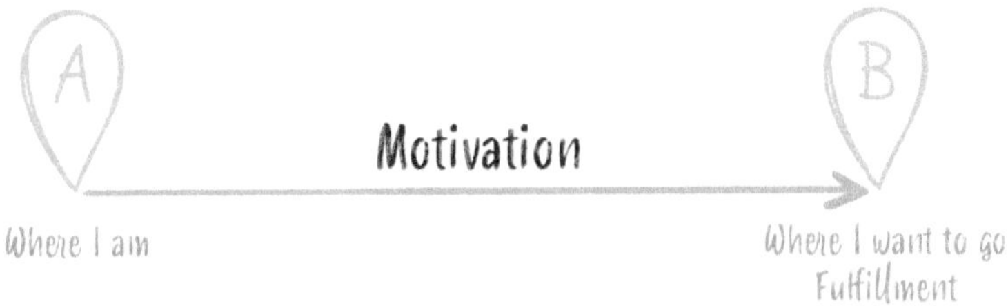

When motivation is generated by the "P objectives" that we've set for ourselves in our path to purpose (which fill our lives with meaning), it is fueled by hope. As it was pointed out when we discussed life's meaning, hope is a disposition elaborated in the appetitive phase, and its contribution to our motivation is enormously powerful, because it helps us stay committed regardless of the hardships we have to endure, and for as long as necessary[140].

Motivation doesn't require an effort to mobilize us. If you're motivated, as soon as you get the opportunity to do that thing that moves you, you will. That's the great thing about intrinsic motivation: it flows, because it's a self-generated process. Unlike those cases were willpower operates.

In that sense, willpower is the ability to do what we must do, despite lacking motivation, feeling displeasure and an internal resistance, employing an effort to achieve it. It can be a great ally when our motivation has faded but we must still persevere to reach our objectives.

For instance, a friend of mine, a well-known Chilean writer, translated his last novel into French. This was a huge challenge, because he knew he couldn't fail. If he succeeded, he would position himself as one of the few Latin American writers to translate their own work into French. But if he failed, his reputation would be diminished in the publishing sphere, but above all before himself. It was a monumental task that took him two years, and not something he particularly enjoyed, as he told me. It required great willpower. Many times, he felt tempted to abandon the project. Only his objective of establishing himself as a bilingual writer made him keep at it and finally overcome this tremendous challenge successfully.

It's as if willpower were our emergency fuel. It's there to help us when we don't particularly feel motivated by a concrete activity that leads to our purpose. However, unlike motivation, which flows without resistance and is inexhaustible, this force seems to be limited, as if we couldn't always be rowing against the current.

If my map isn't working... what could be happening?
We know that if our intention is consistent with the objective we have set for ourselves, we should be on our way. We will be able, then, to activate our intrinsic motivation[141].

But Sheldon has found out in his research that this motivation isn't easy to come by. Often people ignore the objectives that they "should" want or that are good for them, which turns into a significant barrier in our personal development[142]. To understand why this inconsistency is

196

generated, psychology distinguishes between two basic types of cognition[143]:

> - System 1: refers to our unconscious system, involuntary, intuitive, operating almost automatically. Evolutionarily, predates system 2.
>
> - System 2: refers to our conscious process, which requires a mental effort to activate, and which we use to solve more complex scenarios. It is associated with our proactivity, the exercise of freedom or choice and concentration. It is evolutionarily more recent in human beings than system 1.

Sheldon explains that these two systems work, to a great extent, independently from one another, and that System 2 has little access to System 1[144]. What happens, in short, is that our consciousness doesn't have access to all the information about us, and that part which remains unknown is part of System 1 or the subconscious. This hidden information affects our personality and the decisions we make, which leads us to do things without knowing why we're doing them.

Sigmund Freud, known worldwide as the father of psychoanalysis, was the first to develop the existence of the unconscious mind[145]. Phenomena related to hypnosis demonstrated that we can know things without knowing we know them, since we can wish something without knowing why we have that wish. The reference to an unconscious motivation allows us to understand that we are driven by intentions that aren't genuine and that even go against our values.

The above helps us understand that we can only know our authentic intention when we work our consciousness. When we achieve that, we reach the kind of motivation that is tremendously beneficial for us and which leads us to gaining an inherent satisfaction in what we do[146], increases our performance, our ability to innovate, to learn easily, to become involved, be loyal and trusting of others, improving our subjective perception of our well-being. We also manage to commit long-term and persevere, despite difficulties[147].

> ***Sheldon's recommendations to access our motivation are:***
>
> 1/ Following our intuition[148], because it will improve our access to System 1.
>
> 2/ Reflecting[149] on ourselves, so that we're attentive to the subtleties that might be relevant to know ourselves better.
>
> 3/ Being proactive, because it will lead to starting new things, generating changes and focusing in the future in a directed way[150].
>
> 4/ Cultivating our self-esteem, because it's been proved that this type of people takes their own needs and capacities into account when they choose their goals[151].

My friend Josephine

Josephine is one of my best friends. We met at law school and since then we've been inseparable. We've never worked in the same place, so twelve years ago we decided to sacredly meet for lunch on the last Friday of every month. There were two conditions: first, it had to be in an intimate and quiet place, since in that hour and a half we needed to catch up on our most personal things; and second, we had to have a rich chocolate or Nutella dessert.

Josephine is always on time, with her elegant looks, like a New York lawyer. Wearing stilettos and her latest season purse. We became good friends because we share many interests, especially the desire to build a better and fairer society, without discrimination.

We always thought that we would end up working together on something, maybe building our own foundation. However, over the years our dreams and ideals grew apart. Especially after our children were born, because the shift in our priorities and values became more apparent. On our Friday lunches we went from our idealistic conversation to more practical and everyday topics, each time more demanding. Thus, I started feeling Josephine no longer vibrated with life in the same way as before.

Since we turned 35, she became obsessed with a great and ambitious goal: to make partner in her firm as soon as possible, work hard for ten more years, and retire at 45 to then do as she pleased. It sounded like undergoing torture to earn freedom.

Her goal was legitimate, and she also had all the necessary abilities, but the years went by, and not only has she not achieved it yet, but she also looks spiritless and disenchanted with life.

After summer vacations prompted a two-month hiatus in our routine, we resumed it as usual. She was predictably punctual, but looked pale and thinner. When we greeted each other, she gave me a hug that was more affectionate than usual, and sat down staring at me with an exhausted look on her face. Then she said:

—"These have been the worst holidays ever."

—"'Why?— I worriedly asked."

—"I had to work the whole time, didn't get any rest and couldn't enjoy time my children, which was the one thing I wanted."

—"What happened? You couldn't get a sub?"

—"The thing is, if I want to make partner, I can't delegate any of this to other colleagues. Whether you want it or not, in the end we're all competing because only one will make it this year."

That lunch didn't go as the rest did. I felt my friend was having a hard time. It was becoming a recurrent thing since, even though I didn't want to remind her, the same thing had happened last year. That meant two years in a row without a break. We didn't talk again that month, but because I was worried, I suggested changing our next lunch to a Saturday and taking the afternoon off to talk. Just the two of us, rambling for hours, the way we did back in college.

At 1:30 I picked her up from her place and we went to a café to have lunch. Because it was Fall, we were surrounded by Japanese maple leaves scattered all over the ground, just like the ones at my place when we would get together to study. For dessert we had our favorite, pancakes with Nutella and strawberries. We were happy to have that time for ourselves, the one hour and a half lunches always felt too short.

When we were about to order some coffee, Josephine looked at me with sad little eyes, and said: "My friend, I can't take it anymore. Everyone in the office thinks I'm cold and arrogant, there's no one there I can trust, and now that I'm on my way to making partner, I feel it's going to get increasingly harder to have a friendly environment." She told me she had wanted to project that image precisely so that no one would get on her way, and so that they would know she was a determined woman who had clear goals. She added that that was the only way of conducting yourself in a world dominated by men.

I surprised to hear her say that. Josephine was the most caring, generous and maternal person in our group of friends. She was always protecting us, she was completely reliable, brilliant no doubt, persevering, but never intimidating or arrogant. It was as if she were describing someone else.

Right then, I couldn't help but ask her: "Why is making partner so important?" She answered immediately, as if she already had the perfect answered lined up.

—"Because I deserve it. I'm more than qualified, and you know that men much less qualified than me have made it. Also, I would double my salary, which means I could save and in ten years retire to do whatever I wanted to do."

—"And have you been happy through that path? Or do you feel like you will be once you reach your goal?"

This time her answer wasn't immediate. On the contrary, she stopped looking at me and for a second I felt she wouldn't answer the question. But we know each other so well that couldn't avoid it. She stared at the ground for almost a full minute, then raised her head and asked:

—"Does it even matter if I'm happy or not at my job? I set a goal for myself and, as you well know, I won't stop until I get there. That's the way I've always been. It doesn't even cross my mind if it makes me happy or not. My children make me happy. My partner makes me happy. Should my job make me happy too?

Our afternoon was coming to an end, before it got too cold and dark. But suddenly Josephine grabbed my arm and I saw that tears were running down her face. I think in twenty years of friendship I had never seen her cry before. I knew crying for her was tantamount to being vulnerable, and that she would never expose herself like that in public. But something had touched her deeply, even if at the time she still didn't quite understand what.

As it was now late, we went inside the café. We had some tea, Josephine calmed down and she asked me:

—"You know what? Why don't you tell me what I was like in college? I think I've practically forgotten all about it. When I see myself back then, it seems it's a different person altogether."

I reminded her of our strolls down Merced street, when we talked to Isabellísima, the beggar from Lastarria who would share with us theories about the end of the world. Of the bingos we would organize at camp Parcela 4, in Renca, to raise funds for social housing. She herself remembered her dreams of becoming a legislator, and the way I would make fun of her because I used to think politicians didn't do anything. We laughed and cried evoking those years of so many dreams and joys.

Josephine confessed to me that this idealistic and courageous woman of conviction had disappeared between meetings with clients, million dollars mergers and acquisitions, business class trips and tempting end-of-year bonuses. She added that first her father and then her husband had been so sure she would get far, be extremely successful, that she thought by making partner she would meet her own expectations and that of others.

That day many questions came to Josephine's mind, but most importantly, for the first time in decades she gave herself permission to check her motivations and ask herself if that long-cherished desire of making partner, with all the sacrifices and renunciations that it implied, was really the path she wanted for her life.

That same year Josephine lost a loved one. She was not admitted as partner into the law firm and decided to quit.

How does her story end?
Soon after, Josephine started a psychoanalysis process to reconnect with her authentic intention, because she realized that all this time her subconscious had dominated her actions instead of herself. Most likely, this therapy will allow her to start her own path to purpose.

Spoiler Alert! Purpose Wasn't What I Thought It Would Be, But I Discovered So Much More

> *Chase love and you will find happiness. Chase happiness and you will live your purpose".*
>
> Me.

Joe Gardner, the protagonist of Pixar's Soul, is a middle-aged music teacher who once dreamed of becoming a professional jazz player. Because Joe loves playing the piano. As soon as his fingers slide over the keys, a cloud seems to engulf him from the bottom of his shoes and elevate him to an unknown dimension, almost divine, where there's no one else and there's no time. Unfortunately, Joe never followed his dreams and because of his fears he led an apathetic life, very different from the one he wished to have.

Thus, Joe wandered through life numbed, until one afternoon everything changed as suddenly as if he had been struck by lightning. The same day he was presented with the opportunity of a lifetime (to play a jazz concert alongside Dorothea Williams, his idol) a terrible accident puts him in a coma. During this limbo between life and death, Joe tries to escape from the Great Beyond and ends up by mistake in the

Great Before, the universe where souls that haven't been born live. There he meets 22, a young soul known for their incessant efforts to avoid incarnation and coming to the world.

Joe ends up becoming 22's mentor instead of going to the Great Beyond. His mission is to help them find what they're missing to begin a human life: their "spark." Once they find it, they will have a reason to want to live and Joe will be able to go back to Earth in time for his concert.

Joe doesn't want to wait and is willing to do anything to get to his concert. When he is faced with the possibility of death, all that passivity and fear with which he had lived until then, are transformed in a tremendous flow of energy that propels him to achieve his dream. Thus, together with 22, they manage to go back to Earth without the permission of the Great Before's authorities. The outburst comes with a consequence, since they managed to reach the world, but not in their respective bodies. 22's soul lands on Joe's body, whereas Joe's on the body of a cat that was at the foot of his gurney.

In this new scenario, 22, for the first time in a human body, begins exploring earthly life, and feeling emotions, and enjoying the information provided by her senses. In short, to experience all the wonderful and simple things of life, of which no mentor before Joe has ever told her about. For 22, life doesn't seem so fastidious anymore. Gobbling down a delicious slice of pizza, enjoying a conversation with another human being, making others laugh, listening to music while on the subway, watching the leaves fall from the trees because of the wind, or witnessing a reconciliation hug between a mother and a son, are moments of great significance for this young soul.

It is a short expedition, as the pair is discovered by a soul counter and taken back to the Great Before. But the authorities are happy with the outcome of their adventure, because 22 has finally found her spark and can start a human life. However, things don't go, once again, as they should: the moment 22 has to go to earth, she gives Joe her "badge" so that he can return to life. Because of this gesture, he is able to return to his family and fulfill his dreams.

Joe finally gets to play at the jazz concert that he had been so excited about. His performance on stage is glorious, and he is acclaimed by everyone in the audience—his friends, family and jazz fanatics alike. Once the show is over, Joe asks Dorothea, his duo and the jazz player he admires so much: "What comes next?", waiting for something else, as if his dream come true had not been as rewarding as he thought it would be. Dorothea answers: "We'll come back tomorrow and do the same thing. And the day after that. And the day after that." Then he gives Joe a stern look and tells him a story: "I heard this story about a fish. He swims up to this older fish and says:

—I'm trying to find this thing they call the ocean.

—The ocean? That's what you're in right now.— Says the older fish.

—This? This is water. What I want is the ocean!— Says the younger fish.

Right then, Joe feels again that time has stopped and there's no one around him, just as when he slides his fingers over the piano keys. The best memories of his life flash through his mind, as if he were a spectator reviewing his own biography. And he understands 22's spark: Purpose of life is much more than a passion. It can include that passion, but the thing that makes us truly happy is the love we feel for life and everything that exists. Doing things with love. At work, relating to others, while enjoying simple things, while valuing life just because we are alive. Paradoxically, feeling death lurking makes Joe understand purpose of life.

That's the message that Pixar conveys in *Soul*. It might seems like a spoiler for life: that which we were seeking outside, that spark, passion or vocation, is not in the end what we're missing in order to feel complete. It's much simpler than that. And that's what's hopeful about life. When we all start inquiring about purpose, what we seek is that activity or mission that will make us feel fulfilled once we find and exercise it. Some already have it, like Joe, and in those cases it's important to be able to live it. But not all of us have a passion, and that doesn't prevent us from being fully happy. Passion is an element of purpose.

The true spark, common to all human beings, is the power of loving life. The capability of loving everything that exists.

***

What is to love life?

According to St. Thomas Aquinas, "to love is to will the good of the other"; for, Alain, it is "to find one's riches outside oneself"; and to the wise Toltecs, "everything is made of love. Love is life itself". To me, love is the most powerful force there is in the universe. It feels like euphoria inside the chest, occupying all that space that used to be empty. That's why when there's love you feel complete. It is abundance and fullness. The opposite of scarcity.

Eric Fromm points out that "love is an active power in man; a power which breaks through the walls which separate man from his fellow men, which unites him with others". For him, "this desire for interpersonal fusion is the most powerful striving in man. It is the most fundamental passion, it is the force which keeps the human race together, the clan, the family, society"[155]. In the act of loving and giving oneself to someone else, you find yourself and the other, and discover man's true nature.

When people love, they give themselves. But not in a transactional way, where I give something to receive something else. When it comes to love, the mere act of giving brings us joy. In the act itself we experience the strength, richness and vitality of being, and that experience of overflowing vigor fills us with joy. You feel generous, alive and privileged.

This type of love is not the same as romantic love or falling in love (*eros*). It's not the same as family or friendly love either (*philia*).

Love of life goes beyond our close circle or circumstances. It invites us to leave self-love's egotism and narcissism. It is sublime, universal and genuinely selfless. As if it were a form of divine or spiritual love. It is a love that gives by giving it all, not just to close ones but also to strangers, even enemies[156].

It is an altruistic love of humanity, a natural inclination to love man and nature. In scope, it has by far the greatest potential, because it is infinite. Greeks called this kind of love "agape".

> Chase love and you will find happiness.
> Chase happiness and you will live your purpose.

Love is the virtue par excellence. Others, like generosity, humility, justice, empathy, tolerance, collaboration, peace and forgiveness, feed on it. Love opens the way to a life of virtue. It is the food of the human soul.

Finding this kind of love, agape, allows you to stop thinking of yourself as the center of the universe. It gives you the opportunity to challenge your ego each day, and to choose transcendental values over individualistic ones, even if this path always requires more effort. The ego doesn't know how to love, or only loves itself. That's why it wants everything for itself, and yet is never satisfied. Agape is the antidote for this tyranny, because it is a love that's been freed from the ego and frees us from it too. It's the kind of love that must nurture every other types of love.

Because of this form of love, we can go far beyond what we think is possible. We become warriors, prepared to overcome adversity, willing to assume whatever cost. This strength finds little resistance, because it **transforms having-to-do into wanting-to-do**. And when you love, you don't do things out of obligation but because you want to give. Because love is the opposite of duty. That's why I'll take care of nature if I love it. And if I love my job I'll work with pleasure. And if I love my kids, I'll be happy to see them start their own family. If I love my friends, I'll always be there to give them a hand. If I love my country, I'll fight so that our life together is the best possible one. And if I love life, I'll be thankful each day for being alive.

As Kant says, "what is done from constraint is not done from love"[157], which is why Fromm thinks that "the maxim of duty is to act as if you loved."

Unlike other types of love, like that of a couple or between siblings, which rest on feelings, love of life transcends the will and the circumstances, insofar as it rests in an intellection (that is to say, an intellectual understanding that includes the senses) of the world and the universe.

Whoever chooses to follow the path to purpose, does so because they have chosen to love. And love, like purpose, can't be achieved in an instant, it's a journey that never ends and that can get richer and more intense.

Just like with love, purpose holds the remedy for loneliness. We are no longer one, because there's always another with whom that feeling of fusion or unity converges. And it germinates when a person feels that the needs of others are as important as their own[158].

Purpose, happiness and love make up a trilogy where these three elements feed off each other. Purpose of human beings is to be happy, and in order to be happy we need love. Love and happiness create a virtuous circle. The greater the love the greater the happiness and for that reason the level at which we live our purpose increases as well.

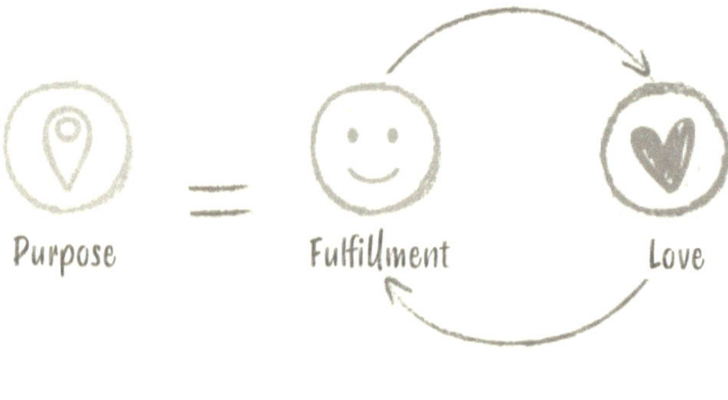

* * *

The freedom to be free

Harriet Tubam, born in 1820 , was an African-American slave who started working for a family in Maryland, the US, when she was five. She would spend the whole day cleaning the house and the stables, and at night she cared for her masters' children. If any of them cried during the one she would be whipped.

One day, when Harriet was seven, tired of the abuse and the whipping, she ran away and hid in a nearby pigsty for five days, eating from the animal feed. Unfortunately, the foreman found her and she was mercilessly whipped upon her return. This episode marked her life profoundly. Since then, she never gave up her intense desire to escape and be free.

Years later, she began working on the cotton plantations. One day, one of the foremen yelled at her harshly and demanded that she whipped another slave working next to her. She refused, and in the midst of the yelling and the fighting, the slave was able to escape. In an attempt to stop the fugitive, the foreman threw a heavy metal weight at him, but hit Harriet on the head instead, leaving her with neurological damage for life. Because of this episode she gained the reputation of a rebellious slave, and was therefore never released.

When she was twenty she was sold to a man with whom she had two kids. Now, not only was she destined for slavery—so were they. So much suffering led her to escape north one summer night in 1849. There she could find her longed-for freedom. Throughout her trip, she was helped by people who opposed slavery and also by the associates of a group called Underground Railroad. These abolitionists had established a series of houses, barns, caves and hideouts for runaway slaves to use on their way to freedom.

Once she was free, Harriet saved money to free more slaves from the south. Until then, when they wanted to run away they would use the North Star for guidance because it pointed north. Harriet would support them by giving them the starting point and the connections, for which she became known as Moses. Like the prophet leading his people from slavery in Egypt to the promised land, she led the slaves to freedom.

She carried out thirteen rescue missions, liberating over three hundred slaves. During the last years of her life, she promoted women's right to vote. When in 1896, the National Federation of Afro-American Women was founded, Harriet Tubman was the keynote speaker.

This story and others give life to the American concept of the North Star, representing the direction that constantly guides our lives towards freedom. It is such a deep and stable direction over time that it remains unaltered by the changes in the world around us.

Why did Harriet dedicate her life to securing the freedom of others, instead of enjoying her own? What she needed was to reach a different level of freedom.

Are We Free?

We think we're free because we have a heap of freedoms whose only limit is respecting other people's rights. We're free to move, think, comment or consume without restrictions. But that truth is that, most of the time, we restrict that freedom ourselves, by living in a mental prison. We stay in romantic relationships that don't satisfy us and do nothing to change that. We work in jobs we hate and have a dream we want to purpue—but are terrified to leave our comfort zone. We forge a gate that prevents us from moving forward, without realizing that there are no barriers right or left. The path is open. It's not a real cell. It's a mental prison.

And so it is with most humans. We feel as if we were incarcerated, but we don't wish to escape our cells because deep down we know that freedom comes with a responsibility. If we were to take responsibility for our role in the world, we would likely realize what needs changing. But people aren't always willing to change. On the contrary, we expect the rest to change. And so we become secondary characters in our own lives, a passive role, waiting for other characters or events to be responsible for the outcome of our film.

Human beings are free when they let themselves choose, not when they're carried away or pushed by the circumstances. Choices make us leave our existential numbness or lethargy, turn attention to ourselves and exercise our freedom in all its magnitude.

Every choice involves changes, in ourselves as much as in our relationship with the world[159]. From the moment we can alter our own present we become free. We can't choose the circumstances that surround us, but we can change the type of relationships we want to have with what is around us. In short, exercising freedom is to persist stubborn but joyously in our chosen direction, no matter the result.

We Are Free to Define Our Success

The Latin word for success, exitus, means exit. It points to the results instead of the doing that gets you there. Achieving what we set out to achieve, our goals and objectives. Our culture teaches us that success means a triumph, beating others, making lots of money and, hopefully, not having to work ever again. But we already know that there's many faces to success, and that material wealth is only one of them. Success is made out of health, energy, enthusiasm about life, close relationships with others, creativity, emotional and psychological stability, a feeling of well-being and peace[160].

Misunderstood success creates a gap in wholeness, and it happens when we put what we are told "we should be" before what we really wish to be. When we're aware of this fracture and how important it is to solve it well, the path to purpose is charged with energy and spiritual love, because we have managed to match what we deeply wish (our intention) with what we do (our objectives). When this happens, everything you do acquires an extraordinary quality, because our activity becomes the channel through which universal consciousness penetrates.

As it can be inferred, there isn't a single path to success, but as many as there are people looking to reach their purpose. Living with purpose, requires that we rediscovered what succeed means to us.

This quote for Ralph Waldo Emerson, is what makes the most sense to me:

*"What is success? To laugh often and much.
To win the respect of intelligent people and the
affection of children; to earn the appreciation
of honest critics and endure the betrayal of
false friends; to appreciate the beauty; to find
the best in others; to leave the world a bit
better, whether by a healthy child, a garden
patch or a redeemed social condition; to know
even one life breathed easier because you have
lived. This is to have succeeded!".*

Ralph Waldo Emerson.

Living with purpose

I started this book wanting to define purpose, and that research paid off, because we found the answers to the following questions:

What is purpose?
Something or someone's reason for existing.

What is purpose of human beings?
Happiness

However, during the process I realized that this was not what was truly valuable. What was valuable was the discovery of something else: how to live with purpose or what is that purpose path.

Purpose is, ultimately, a life philosophy, guiding us to organize it in a way that will make us happy.

We set objectives and goals for ourselves that reflect who we are and our place in the world. This process can't take place before we deeply delving and reflecting about our authenticity and our passions, making sense out of the different objectives and goals that we set for ourselves. And always keeping in mind that in each of them we must be contributing to something bigger than ourselves.

Thus, from now on, instead of asking ourselves or others, what's your purpose?, we should ask:

> *Do you know your path to purpose?*
> *What are your "P objectives"?*
> *Do you live with purpose?*

Purpose is:

"A life philosophy that guides us into living according to our own authentic intention, and transcendental objectives."

When we succeed in living with purpose we achieve the three impacts of the *telos:*

1/ Transforming our values into more transcendental ones;

2/ Activating our intrinsic motivation; and

3/ Finding that happiness that we were looking for based on love

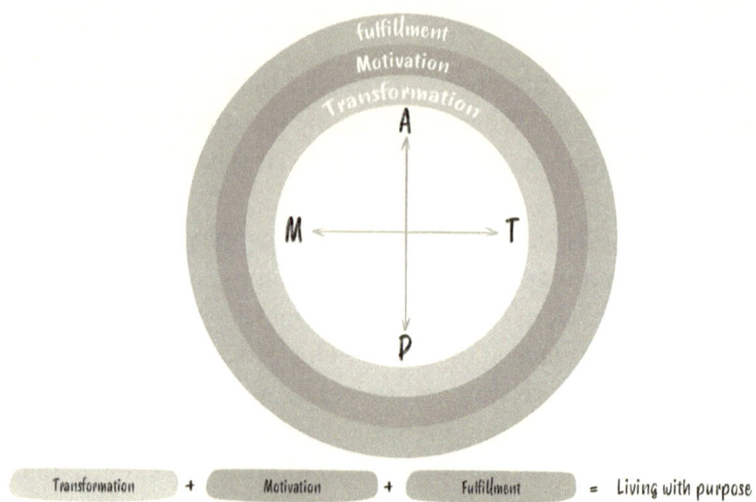

So why not say it like that from the start?

If you had not traveled the path to purpose from the start, what was said in this chapter would only be empty words blown by the wind. You must remember that we're complex beings; the more the look for what we want, the less we get it. Sometimes the short cut won't do it and we have to take the longer road.

That's what the laws of the universe say, according to philosopher Alan Watts: the more you search for happiness, the less satisfied you are—because by chasing it directly, you only strengthen that which you lack. The more you want to be rich, the poorer and more insignificant you feel, no matter how much money you really have. The more you desperately want to be happy or loved, the lonelier and more fearful you'll get—no matter who's around you.

That's why we don't just become happy overnight. Happiness, by seeking to belong, and through self-realization and transcendence, will stick its head along the way.

Nor can we pretend to be always happy, because life isn't about that. We will always face problems that need solving. The challenge isn't about avoiding them and looking for an easy life, but rather in **finding those problems that we do enjoy solving or are willing to suffer for.**

Effort and sacrifice are part of a life of purpose. Paradoxically, it is the pain after exercising which makes us stronger; stumbling after starting something new teaches us what's necessary to succeed; being aware of our ego keeps it in check; facing difficult but honest conversations makes relationships grow[161]. Sacrifice (understood as the delay of a gratification) is biologically useful to our survival and to bring change about. It's time to stop looking at it as if it were a bad thing.

Anyway... I could go on and on about purpose. But nothing I say will be more useful than what my children taught me by telling me the story of the invisible bucket.

Have You Filled Your Bucket Today?

One night of quarantine because of the pandemic, when I could no longer think of anything to entertain my daughters, they suggested we play a game. It consisted of asking tough questions and, if anyone knew their answers, they would win a prize. I accepted. But because I didn't have any prize to give, I thought I would ask such complex questions that they would never know their answers. I usually talk to them about purpose, so that they can be involved in what I do, and above all I try to transmit the value that it will have in their lives as adults. I took advantage of that and I asked them:

—"What is purpose?"

My oldest daughter, Nicole, who's ten, looked at me with that know-it-all face she gets when she's sure of something:

—"Mom, we all have an invisible bucket. We can't see it but it's there. It has a very special function: to keep the good thoughts and feelings about ourselves. It feels good when it's filled, because it makes us happy. And we feel sad and alone when it's empty."

The eight-year-old, Emilia, and Amanda, who's six, began interrupting, as if they knew what was coming next. But Nicole, as a good older sister, managed to silence them and continued:

"Your bucket fills up when you do something to fill someone else's. For example, when you show affection or do something nice for them. Also by being respectful, smiling at them, making them feel special. That's purpose, mom! Like when you hug me when I'm sad, or spend time with me when I'm feeling lonely."

Emilia added:

—"If you try to empty someone else's bucket, by bothering them or making them feel bad, to fill your own, it won't work. If you hurt other people or bully them, you bucket will remain empty."

And Amanda said at last:

—"What matters is filling other people's buckets, only that way you can fill your own."

My three daughters knew this story. So far it is the clearest, simplest and most pedagogical explanation of how to live with purpose that I know[162].

What will you do to fill your bucket from now on?

* * *

END

CONSCIOUSNESS:
THIS IS WHAT I HAVE LEARNED SO FAR ABOUT PURPOSE

Telos **Test**

Now that you are an purpose expert go ahead and take this test to measure the level of purpose in each sphere of your life.

APPENDIX

Appendix I: *Ikigai and the Golden Circle*

Ikigai: a Japanese millennial philosophy

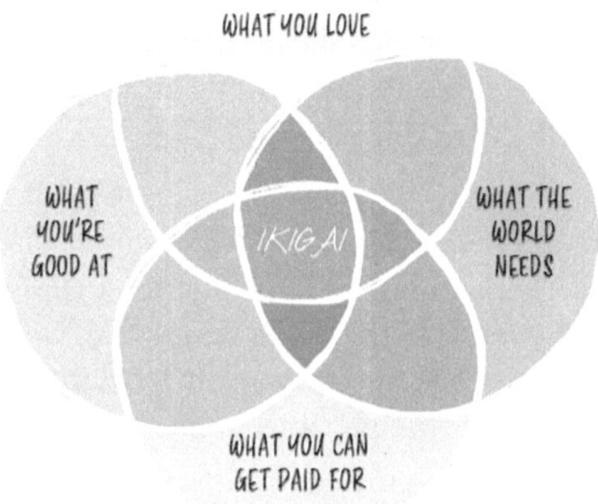

In Asia, the Japanese created their own philosophy of purpose, known as *ikigai*, which translated to English means someone's reason for being or existing. Different authors have developed this concept for the western world, emphasizing that *ikigai* philosophy seeks to answer existential questions such as:

What's that which is worth living for?

What's that which makes us want to get up in the morning?

What's that which pleases us and makes us feel alive?

Ikigai has a holistic approach to life which looks for a balance between the physical, the mental and the spiritual. For that it considers the importance of interpersonal relationships, contributing to a better world, healthy eating, exercising and doing what we love[163].

This philosophy became popular in the West in the early 21st century, after National Geographic researched the regions of the world where people lived the longest. The study pointed its readers' antennas towards Okinawa, Japan, one of the five places (*the Blue Zones*) mentioned in the article[164].

The island, located in the southern part of Japan, has not only been recognized worldwide for the longevity of its inhabitants, but also because their health conditions are better than the world average. This phenomenon has been attributed to a high standard of life, based on this holistic view of human existence and the life of purpose they lead.

Elements that make up ikigai

In recent times, the Japanese philosophy's contribution that has transcended the most is perhaps the diagram of ikigai. It is presented as a drawing describing the four fundamental elements that, in its view, constitute purpose of a person.

a) What you love

b) What the world needs

c) What you're good at, or your talents

d) What you can get paid for[165].

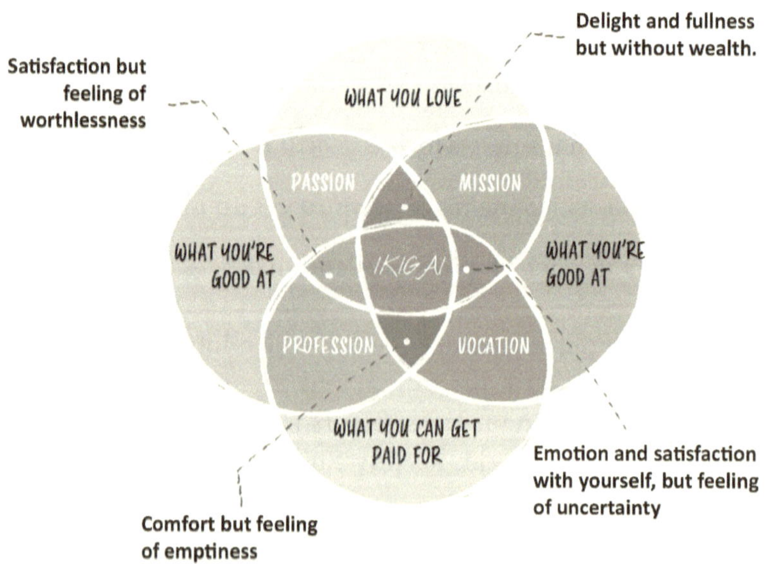

This classic diagram represents the four elements of ikigai or purpose, and the effect produced by their different combinations.

According to ikigai, these four elements combine in different ways[166]. For every two elements combined, a new concept emerges[167]:

> **Profession,** from combining "what you're good at" and "what you can get paid for."
>
> **Vocation,** from combining "what the world needs" or what I can contribute and "what you can get paid for."
>
> **Mission,** from combining "what the world needs" and "what you love."
>
> **Passion,** from combining "what you're good at" and "what you love."

Surely, when you were little people asked you many times what you wanted to be when you grew up, mentioning different professions or vocations pursued by relatives or acquaintances, but never mentioning a mission or passion. That's because in western culture a successful professional life generates wealth, and the importance of a passion or a mission is relegated, because they not considered financially sustainable paths.

As far as we can remember, we are encouraged and challenged to find a vocation or profession that will determine, to a great extent, our identity and value in society. Because of this, usually those who show passion or a sense of determination (for instance, when it comes to artistic or altruistic occupations) are told to consider it a hobby and not their main activity, the belief being that they won't be able to support themselves. This has led us to have a practical view of life, leaving aside a more complete and transversal view of human development, which does include passions and missions.

On the contrary, ikigai is wise to recognize that life is more complex and goes beyond a profession, vocation, mission or passion. Likewise, it establishes that purpose will only be reached once the four fundamental elements are combined. Obviously, the ideal is to maintain a balance between the four, even when in most cases some elements are lived with greater intensity than others[168]. For example, if my job consists of working with homeless people, the element of "what I love doing" will likely be more prevalent than "what I can get paid for," and the same goes with living a life of purpose, as long as that predominance is consistent with our desires and meets our needs.

Ikigai also shows what happens in an intermediate phase, for instance, when we reach three out of the four elements. As a result, different sensations emerge that prevent the subject from feeling complete, despite being close to reaching their purpose, because he is lacking one of them. That's why the emerging sensation will depend on the missing element from our combination, and could give rise to a feeling of worthlessness, emptiness, uncertainty or poverty.

Simon Sinek and the Golden Circle

In recent years, acclaimed author and inspirational speaker Simon Sinek has made purpose popular through his TED talks, videos on social networks and his fascinating books on the whys of people or companies[169]. His communicational efforts have been extraordinarily helpful in generating awareness on purpose among a younger and massive audience. For Sinek, the why (or purpose) is our reason for being or existing.

One of his most influential presentations took place when he presented the Golden Circle, which aims to explain the differences between the why, the how and the what of the things we do, the first being the most important dimension and, according to what Sinek teaches us, the way in which we truly connect with others.

Sinek also explained in an extremely simple way something very complex to understand: the way our brain operates, first proposed in 1960 by neuroscientist Paul MacLean from Yale University. With a simple image, and a brief explanation, he showed that our frontal cortex is the part of the brain that handles our reasoning and language, whereas the limbic brain is the part in charge of our emotions. Sinek believes that the limbic brain lacks language, which explains why we have a hard time expressing our feelings.

This is important, because the philosophy of purpose that we're introducing here seeks precisely to help us deal with our incapacity to understand and handle our emotions, by naming those things we feel but are incapable of expressing verbally.

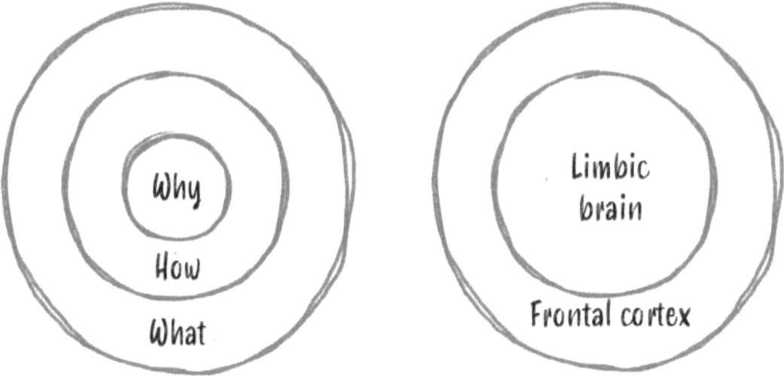

These images show that the "why" of the things we do and the "how" we do them are within the scope of the limbic brain, our emotional part; whereas the "what" obeys the frontal cortex, the rational area of the brain.

Appendix II: Definitions of purpose

The following table covers the definitions of purpose created by different authors, and which were used to create the *telos* philosophy.

Author	Definition of purpose	Key Elements
Viktor Frankl (1963), *Man's Search for Meaning*	There is a unique and individual talent, different for each of us, which gives meaning to existence.	Individuality and meaning
Martin Seligman (2012), *Flourish: A Visionary New Understanding of Happiness and Well-being.*	Belonging and serving something which we believe is bigger than ourselves.	Transcendence
Carol Ryff (1989), *"Happiness is Everything, or Is It? Exploration on the Meaning of Well-being[170]"*.	Sense of direction in life.	Direction
Todd B. Kashdan and **Patrick E. McKnight** (2009), *"Origins of Purpose in Life: Refining our Understanding of a Life Well Lived[171]"*.	Central and self-organizing life objective which allows you to prioritize and motivate yourself towards goals, regulate behaviors and provide a sense of meaning.	Direction and meaning
Corey Keyes (2011), *"Authentic Purpose: The Spiritual Infrastructure of Life[172]"*.	The quality of being determined to make or achieve a constructive goal for a group of people.	Transcendence
Aaron Hurst (2014), *Purpose Economy.*	Purpose lives in the intersection between what makes sense to us and the impact we wish to generate.	Transcendence and values

Gary T. Reker and Paul T. P. Wong (1988), *Aging as an individual process: Toward a Theory of Personal Meaning.*	The knowledge of the order, consistency and reason behind your own existence; the pursuit and achievement of worthwhile goals, and the consequent sense of accomplishment.	Direction, meaning and values
William Damon (2008), *The Path to Purpose: Helping Our Children Find Their Calling in Life.*	Purpose in life is a stable and widespread intention that gives our lives meaning, while allowing us to contribute to something greater than ourselves.	Intention, direction and transcendence
John Battista and Richard Almond (1973), *"The Development of Meaning in Life*[173]*";* **Gary T. Reker and Paul T. P. Wong** (1988), *"Meaning and Purpose in Life and Well-being: a Life-span Perspective*[174]*".*	Consistency with life.	Meaning
James Crumbaugh and Leonard Maholick (1964), *"An Experimental Study in Existentialism: The psychometric approach to Frankl's concept of noogenic neurosis*[175]*".*	Ontological meaning of life from the perspective of an individual who experiences.	Meaning, doing
Login S. George and Crystal L. Park (2013), *"Are Meaning and Purpose Distinct? An Examination of Correlates and Predictors*[176]*".*	The point of having central goals, a direction in life and enthusiasm in relation to the future.	Direction, goals and motivation

Appendix III: Abraham Maslow's Theory Z[177]

Abraham Maslow developed this theory about the characteristics of transcendent people, understood as those who live their purpose:

1. For those who achieve a state of transcendence, peak and plateau (or mystical) experiences become the most important thing in their lives.
2. The language of being, poets, mystics, seers, and deeply spiritual people comes easy to them, natural and unconsciously.
3. They perceive the world around them as a unity and a holiness (in a secular sense) which encompasses all things in an everyday way.
4. They are aware of and especially motivated by transcendent values, like truth, beauty, goodness, unity and sense of wonder.

My Friends From purpose 

5. They seem to somehow recognize each other with other transcendent beings, reaching an intimacy and mutual understanding even the first time they meet.
6. They are more sensitive to beauty, not necessarily in conventional terms, and present a tendency to embellish things.
7. They have a more holistic view of life. Cultural, religious, political or intellectual prejudices or differences practically cease to exist and are easily overcome. Tend to view all human beings as equal.
8. They have a natural tendency to achieve synergies between different groups. They aren't governed by the competition paradigm, but rather by collaboration, where you don't seek to win or lose, but to maximize the benefit for all.

9. It is easier for them to overcome their own ego, making way for a life lived according to their authentic identity.

10. They are lovable people, inspiring, less earthly or purer, and so others see them as great human beings.

11. They are more innovative and curious. They have a vision of the future, of what's ideal, of what we could become, and therefore of human potential.

12. Although they experience more moments of ecstasy, excitement, and fullness, they're likely less happy (in a hedonic sense) than self-realized people who don't seek to transcend. That's because their sensitivity makes them feel a kind of sadness by perceiving so clearly the self-destruction, cruelty and the lack of perspective that characterizes human stupidity. Maslow claims that this is the price to pay for such a clear vision of the world's beauty, the possibilities of human nature and the absence of evil.

13. They distance themselves from the inherent elitism of any competitive culture, which makes a privileged group feel superior to others. This is possible because they conceived each person as an equally spiritual being, connected to themselves, an equal despite their differences.

14. They show more strongly a positive correlation between increased knowledge and the sense of wonder, since they're curious and humble at the same time.

15. They have an easier time spotting creative and virtuous people.

16. They understand and accept the existence of evil as part of the universal balance. This grants them a better understanding of the concept, as well as greater compassion and acceptance when faced with it.

17. They see themselves as intermediaries or temporary custodians of something bigger than themselves. While they acknowledge their talents and develop their whole potential for intelligence, efficiency, creativity, leadership and spirituality, by being aware of their ego they usually don't have arrogant attitudes.

18. Most of them are religious or spiritual people.
19. While they can have a strong character and be very clear about who they are, where they're going, what they want and what they're good for, they also know it's not about them and go way beyond their own identity.
20. They easily marvel at the simple things in life and appreciate them just the way they are.
21. They know how to live a full life, giving themselves completely to love and without conflicts.
22. They love their work, and in general look for an activity that can merge that which they are with what they do. They see money as a means to live and not an end in itself. They prefer simplicity and don't seek luxuries, privileges, honors or material possessions.
23. They identify more with Sheldon's ectomorphic somatotype.

Appendix IV: Levels of Transcendence

Flow

Flow is a mental state of absorption while focusing on an interesting and challenging task. Under a state of flow, the self fades as it merges with the activity. Afterwards, consciousness re-emerges, enriched by the experience.

Mindfulness

Mindfulness is the human capacity to be fully present, aware of where we are and what we're doing. We all have this capacity, but we need to learn how to access it. One of its benefits is that it allows us to lower our reactive behavior and the overwhelming feeling about what's happening around us. It allows to see life without prejudice, removing the negative thoughts from our mind, connecting us with our most spiritual values, like detachment, open-mindedness, compassion, empathy, consciousness and altruism[178].

Gratitude[179]

Gratitude has been described as an attitude, an emotion, a state of mind, a moral virtue, a habit, a motif, a personality trait, a coping response, and even a way of life.

The important thing is to know that gratitude is the acknowledgment of kindness in our own life, and it has elements that make the joy of living it worthwhile. Being aware that we have received something gratifies us, either by its presence or by the effort of those who gifted it to us. It's also about discovering that the sources of kindness lie, at least partially, outside ourselves. The object of gratitude is always directed at someone else: people, God, nature, never to oneself.

Gratitude implies humility, the recognition that we couldn't be who are today or be where we are in life without the contribution of others. By being grateful we feel good, and we are motivated to share the kindness we have received with others.

Sense of Wonder

It is a positive emotion that includes significant perceptible changes; for instance, altering the sense of time[180]. It can be the result of perceiving the vastness surrounding us and needing to accommodate to it[181]. This vastness can take a perceptual form, such as watching the Northern Lights, or conceptual, such as encountering for the first time a theory that seems to explain almost everything[182]. It is, then, a reaction when we find ourselves in front of some aspect of the world that amazes us.

Inspiration

It's a state characterized by the production of a high intellectual activation, clarity, openness and attraction towards an object, accompanied with a pleasant feeling[183].
This state is characterized by three elements:

1/ Evocation: it is experienced as a reaction to an outside stimulus or one that arises from an intrapsychic source (for instance, memory or unconscious processes). The inspired subject doesn't feel directly responsible for this state, although he might feel responsible for creating the favorable conditions for it to happen.

2/ Transcendence: we understand that the evoking object reveals new or better possibilities, and the individual acquires a new cognitive consciousness of that possibility.

3/ Motivation: the subject is directed to seek a positive outcome instead of avoiding a negative one, and feels motivated to carry out the new or better ideas[184].

Altruistic Actions

Altruism comes from the French word altruism, meaning the willingness to seek the good of others, even at the expense of your own. Its most frequent forms are volunteering, whereby you dedicate your time to an activity that's not remunerated for a socially valuable cause; and donations, through which you give others a material good, typically a sum of money, without expecting anything in return. It can be a pound of sugar or a large sum of money, what matters is the intention and not the good donated, as well as the degree of involvement.

Service Vocation

This is a widely used concept when referring to dedication in the workplace. Even though it's usually mixed with purpose, it is more specific. Vocation is the meaning we get from working in what we love doing, where we can use our talents and, at the same time, improve the pains that seem to ail the world[185].

Service vocation is a virtue that allows us to express love for others. It lies in the field of action, of doing something for someone else. It's an attitude of the spirit by which we open ourselves to a world which is rich in experiences. And where we can get the best out of ourselves while, in turn, enriching our consciousness with these relationships.

Putting yourself at the service of others implies an authentic process of connection between both parties—the one who serves and the one who is served. This connection will in time take the form of a relationship that allows those who serve to put a number of virtues into practice, which will in turn enable their own self-realization and transcendence. The most common forms of service are religious and work.

Generativity

According to Erik Erikson's theory of psychosocial development[186], generativity is the challenge we face in middle age. It is defined as the interest in guiding and ensuring the well-being of future generations, leaving a legacy that will survive us. Generativity can be expressed through activities like raising children, caring for disabled people, or forming young people.

In any case, it implies a contribution to the common good of the environment in which we belong, strengthening and enriching social institutions, ensuring a continuity between generations, proposing social improvements. This element is intimately connected with what we leave behind in this earthly world, our legacy. It responds, no more, no less, to the moral duty of leaving this world better than how we found it.

Love

As human beings, we feed our consciousness with love. When we are little, we need to receive it from our parents; as adults, in a reciprocal way with those closest to us. Then, a time comes when our capacity to love expands without limits, and the desire is born to give love to any human being, even if we don't know them. Love initially satisfies our needs of belonging and connection, but it is also a source of energy to positively impact the life of others. In any of its forms, it invites us to transcend and it is possibly the most powerful way to do so.

Mystical Experiences: Peak and Plateau

Peak experiences, as Maslow points out, are those in which we transcend our personal concerns. In such revealed aesthetic or emotional states, we feel an intense joy, peace, well-being and an awareness of the ultimate truth and unity of all things[187]. When we live them, a feeling emerges that new horizons and possibilities are opening up for ourselves and others.

When these peak experiences become more permanent, they are called plateau or mystical experiences, which are more lasting, serene and cognitive. In this state, besides feeling a kind of ecstasy, we also perceive a gist of sadness, when we realize that others can't experience similar encounters. While Maslow believed that mature, self-realized people were more likely to have these experiences, he also pointed out that everyone in the world can have them.

For Maslow, when we transcend we enter a state in which we stop worrying about trifles, and we can focus on what is truly important: living a virtuous life.

According to Romain Rolland, by transcending, personal problems become trivial, and for a few moments our body is filled with an unusual beatific pleasure. Rolland described this experience as a feeling of eternity, as something without limits or barriers, as a feeling of vastness and completeness. There are several other authors who have tried to describe this type of experience, although the vast majority recognize that it is practically impossible to do so with the exact language.

They are transformations that are felt intensely and that stick with us. While the moment itself is fleeting, it reaches the innermost part of our being, because it penetrates our deepest layers of consciousness, beyond what's apparent and superficial. In some cases, this is revealing, as it provides us with the solution to a problem that we long to solve, or it leads us to a new discovery. Without a doubt, it is a experience which enriches our life, changes the direction of our goals, and, above all, makes us feel that our life has a purpose.

Many agree on one thing: the most profound mystical experiences come from those moments in which we overcome a struggle or challenged that seemed almost impossible to overcome or reach. When we see that we are capable of incredible things, we begin to lose that fear that was preventing us from growing. For Maslow, the issue of effort is crucial to our well-being: it is not about achieving something, but about striving for it[188].

Table 1

This table shows sources or life meaning according to different well-known authors on the subject.

	BELONGING / FAMILY	SELF-REALIZATION / ACHIEVEMENTS	TRANSCENDENCE / RELIGION / SPIRITUALITY	WORK	COMMUNITY	POLITICS	RECREATION
ROBERT A. EMMONS (1999), *"PERSONAL GOALS, LIFE MEANING, AND VIRTUE: WELLSPRINGS OF A POSITIVE LIFE*[189]*"*.	X	X	X				
PAUL T. P. WONG AND PREM S. FRY (1998), *THE HUMAN QUEST FOR MEANING: A HANDBOOK OF PSYCHOLOGICAL RESEARCH AND CLINICAL APPLICATIONS*[190].	X	X	X				
KAREN L. DEVOGLER AND PETER EBERSOLE (1998), *"ADULTS' MEANING IN LIFE*[191]*"*.	X		X	X	X	X	
KENDALL COTTON BRONK (2013), *PURPOSE IN LIFE: A CRITICAL COMPONENT OF OPTIMAL YOUTH DEVELOPMENT*[192].	X	X	X	X	X		
CAROL D. RYFF AND BURTON SINGER (1998), *"THE CONTOURS OF POSITIVE HUMAN HEALTH*[193]*"*.	X			X			X
GERBEN WESTERHOF, ERNST BOHLMEIJER, AND MARIJE W. VALENKAMP (2004), *"IN SEARCH OF MEANING: A REMINISCENCE PROGRAM FOR OLDER PERSONS*[194]*"*.	X	X	X	X	X	X	X

Glossary:

Agape: the highest form of love, felt for everything that exists in the universe by the mere fact of being a part of it.

Authenticity: value that refers to someone who tells the truth, accepts responsibility for their feelings and behavior, and is sincere and consistent with themselves and others. It can also be expressed as the fidelity to oneself, spirit and character.

Path to purpose: life as a unique journey for each person, which evolves with our own development.

Consciousness: human capacity to perceive reality and recognize themselves in it.

Spirituality: intuition that leads us to feel and understand that we are all connected to each other by something bigger than ourselves, beyond any dogma or belief.

Eudaimonia: happiness in its full sense, containing the pleasure and meaning of life. Also called "happiness," "flourishing," or "well-being."

Hedonism: a form of happiness which focuses on seeking pleasure and moving away from pain.

Intention: our will's determination towards a goal.

Personal map: a way to organize and visualize our path to purpose. It allows us to incorporate purpose, our objectives and goals into our life plan.

Goal: objective that seeks short or medium-term results, allowing us to generate a life plan and feel like we're making progress in a certain direction.

Motivation: energy that moves us to achieve what we're interested in.

Objective: where life is headed in a specific area.

Passion: strong inclination towards an activity or cause that we love and that we're good at.

Meaning of life: intellectual capacity that allows us to perceive ourselves in our own uniqueness, and intimately understand the life that deserves to be lived.

Oceanic Feeling: a concept referring to the fact that we are part of a larger whole. Like a drop in the ocean, where we're each a drop and the ocean is the universe.

Telos ("Purpose" in Greek): methodology that aims to help people find their path to purpose. It is made up of four elements: authenticity, passion, meaning of life and transcendence. It generates three impacts on people's lives: it transforms their values, it activates their intrinsic motivation, and it allows them to achieve happiness.

Transcendence: the desire to contribute to something bigger than ourselves.

Virtue: human quality which defines doing good.

ACKNOWLEDGMENTS

One of the main reasons for writing this book was to say thank you. Thousands of times I have thought about the way of putting into words feeling as deep as gratitude. By saying thank you, we bare our humility in public. It is a way of acknowledging that we couldn't be ourselves without the contribution of others. Being grateful doesn't mean giving recognition away to favor others. It is a way of transcending.

I have learned that great works cannot exist by an individual effort. Life is too complex for that. If there is something great about this work, and I hope there is, I owe it to those I'll mention below.

I'll start with my family, by blood and extended:

To my husband Diego

The most authentic part of my life. Because of you I learned what love and freedom are.

This book was our way of communicating and sharing something very deep. The greatest proof of our love was your generosity in giving me the space to live this process.

You gave me the idea, the shot in the arm, were my main and unconditional editor and also came up with the title that after several months we chose for this essay.

This book is, without a doubt, our fourth child.

To my daughters Nicole, Emilia and Amanda.

You made me learn that love is the most powerful force in the universe.

I feel on my back the responsibility of setting an example for you. I long for you to be free and compassionate women, pursuing your dreams, but also knowing that happiness is a job that lasts a lifetime.

I've managed to let go. I'm certain that for you to see me complete, as I am today, that's the best lesson I can give you. I know there's been a high price paid in time, but having lived through this together will mark our relationship forever.

I love that you think I'm crazy. I hope we do many crazy things together. You're everything to me.

Eli, if we didn't have you by our side, I would've never dared do this. You've cared for my daughters as if they were your own, and no words are enough to thank you for that.

To the women that have inspired me

To my grandmother Ester, Muma. You have been my partner and the most unconditional person in my life. I confirmed all my hypotheses about happiness with you. You taught me that material things only make sense when you share them; that what matters is people's trust and not recognition; that a deep conversation is worth more than a luxurious trip; that many times loving can be painful, but that a life without love is not worth living. You made me truly understand what *Eudaimonia* is.

To my grandmother Olgui, may she rest in peace. You sowed the seed in me, and the seed ran its natural course once you left. Because of that, I've never let you go. Something of yours is still in me. You have transcended in me.

To my parents.

For giving me my life. I feel free today and I can love you regardless of what might happen. I hope that when you read this book you get to know me from a different place, one I haven't been able to share with you.

To my siblings Nicky and Jonathan.

You were both an inspiration for this book. Each of you represents a side of success.

Nicky, I admire your perseverance. The world is waiting for you to put all your talents at the service of something even bigger. I can imagine this book will have you questioning many things that you've been thinking about for a while. Hopefully, I can inspire you to set your new objectives.

Jonathan, you certainly have an idea of success that others can't wrap their heads around. But suddenly I was able to see it—you have found your inner peace. I will be forever grateful that it was you who brought me closer to the power of consciousness. I didn't write your story in this book because you deserve your own. I miss your physical presence, but I feel deeply connected to you every day of my life.

To my in-laws, Esther and Óscar.
Everything flows with you, because you only know how to give without asking for anything in return.
You made me learn that you build the life you want to live, and that we have the power of deciding what family we want to start.

To Andrea, my sister-in-law.
She's been with me through every minute of this process, with that selfless altruism that characterizes her..

To my best friends: my "Yayas.".
If anyone's witnessed my change, it's been you. You've listened and contained me from the start. You know me better than anyone else, because we've never been afraid of being ourselves when we're together. Those who say that women are jealous and competitive have never had a true friendship like ours. Without you, I would've never dared: LyC

To César, Francisco, Renzo and my PwC family.
Life gives you people who guide you, give you their wisdom and trust. You have paved the way for me and traveled it with me. You've made PwC a home, and are part of my family.
A message to all leaders: know that your actions can change the lives of those you lead.

To the great team that made this possible.
To my editor and writing teacher, Mauricio Electorat. You managed to channel my anxiety and emotions. We're reached our desired result, and much more: we've enjoyed the process and this exercise became my therapy during the Covid-19 lockdown.
To Joan Melé, for generously and humbly writing the foreword to my book.
Iván Armijo, thank you for helping me validate my thesis on the *telos* statistically. Your work confirmed that this book isn't about a hunch or my personal experience, but empirically true.
To Pablo Sepúlveda, my close friend. I'll always be thankful for having me introduced to the world of purpose. I feel that we've written this book together.

All my love and admiration for Eli Rudnick and Andrés B., my spiritual guides and mentors.

To Camila Salas and Carolina Faget for designing my emotions, and to EBook Patagonia for the book's interior design. Also to Giovi Bacchi and Belab for the cover design.

To Ángeles Quinteros, for looking at the smallest detail so that the final edition could be perfect. To my dear friend Trinidad Vicuña for proof-reading and improving many of the stories in this book.

To Andrea Sierra for supporting me with the commercial pitch. To Alan Weschler, for supporting me just like that, because he believed in my cause.

To my friends from purpose

To all those people that purpose put on my way. Within minutes of meeting you, it already felt like our friendship had lasted a lifetime. You've confirmed to me that Maslow's Theory Z exists, and you have filled me with joy throughout the journey.

Joan Melé · **Coni Alveal** · Julia Arana · *Nacha Blanco*
Anna Bonan · Sam Cohen · **JUAN CARLOS CORVALÁN**
Dante Aguirre · *Pabla Flores* · Tomás Lawrence · Ignacio Loyola
Damián Gelerstein · **Miry Kuperman** · Vivi Giacaman
Jonathan Chernilo · **Alfredo Zepeda** · Fabián Schiaffino
Patrick Humpreys · **HANS ROSENKRAZ** · J. Larenas · Delfina Lawson
Felipe León · **Cata Littin** · Rafa Rodríguez · Pato Mayr
María Eugenia López · Caro Contreras · **Josefa Monge**
Fran Egaña · **Nico Morales** · Kathy Muller · Matías Rojas
Jeannette V. W. · **Adolfo Numi** · Trini Vicuña · Pablo Sepúlveda
Nelson Rodríguez · **Juan Carlos Obrador** · Adiel Oros
Gonzalo Pérez · Juan Ignacio Pitta · **GUILLERMO CABALLERO**
Ale Pizarro · **Paulina Robles** · RODRIGO SAA · **Javier Sanfeliú**
Vero Torres · **Cristián Walker** · Evelyn Stevens

Rosh Hashanah Jewish Prayer

Tribute to the mystery of life that welcomes, embraces and blesses us.

May your awakenings wake you up.
And that when you wake up, may you always get excited about this new day.
May the sun rays that shine through your window into each new dawn never become routine.
And may you have the clarity of seeing and rescuing the most positive of each person that crosses your path.
May you not forget to taste the food you eat, carefully, even if it is "only" bread and water.
May you find some time during the day, even if it's short and brief, to raise your eyes to the sky and say thank you, for the miracle of health, that mysterious and beautiful internal balance.
May you manage to express the love you feel for your loved ones.
And may your arms embrace.
And may your kisses kiss.
And may the sunsets surprise you, and never cease to amaze you.
May you arrive tired and satisfied at nightfall from the task you've done during the day.
And may your dream be calm, restful and without fear.
May you not confuse your work with your life, nor the value of things with their price.
And may you not believe yourself more than anyone, because only the ignorant do not know that we are nothing but dust and ash.
And may you not forget, for a moment, that every second of life is a gift, and that, if we were really brave, we would dance and sing with joy when we became aware of it.

QUOTES

FOREWORD

1. www.sistemab.org and www.bcorporation.net.

CHAPTER II: Happiness

2. Baumeister, R. F.; Vohs, K. D.; Aaker, J. L. and Garbinsky, E. N. (2013). "Some Key Differences Between a Happy Life and a Meaningful Life". *The Journal of Positive Psychology* 8(6), p. 505-516. Retrieved from http://dx.doi.org/10.1080/17439760.2013.830764.

3. Sarva Siddhanta Sangraha of Sankaracarya, stanzas 9-12.

4. Waterman, A. S. (1984). *The Psychology of Individualism.* Praeger.

5. Huta, V. and Ryan, R. M. (2010). "Pursuing Pleasure or Virtue: The differential and Overlapping Well-being Benefits of Hedonic and Eudaimonic Motives". *Journal of Happiness Studies: An Interdisciplinary Forum on Subjective Well-Being* 11(6), p. 735-762. Retrieved from https://doi.org/10.1007/s10902-009-9171-4.

6. Ben-Shahar, T. (2007). *Happier: Learn the Secrets to Daily Joy and Lasting Fulfillment.* McGraw Hill.

7. While the author has received criticism for not justifying his claims scientifically, more recent theories, like neuroscientist Britt Andreatta's, have followed a similar line of thought, classifying them into needs of survival, belonging and self.

8. It has been erroneously said that, in order to move into a higher level, the preceding need must be fully satisfied. This was discarded by Maslow himself, in his last studies, where he points out that it is possible to move into higher needs without the previous ones being satisfied— except of course when it comes to the basic ones.

9. Goldstein, K. (2000). *The Organism.* Zone Books.

10. Maslow, A. H., Frager, R., Fadiman, J., McReynolds, C., y Cox, R. (1987). *Motivation and Personality.* Longman.

11. See Appendix II with its references to different authors and their definitions for purpose.

12. Diener, E. (2000). "Subjective well-being: The Science of Happiness and a Proposal for a National Index". *American Psychologist 55*, p. 34-43.

13. Seligman, M. E. P. (2012). *Flourish: A Visionary New Understanding of Fulfillment and Well-being*. Atria Books. / Seligman, M. E. P. (2004). *Authentic Happiness: Using the New Positive Psychology to Realize Your Potential for Lasting Happiness*. Atria Books.

14. Ben-Shahar, T.; *loc. cit.* p. 40.

15. Zak, P. (2017). *Trust Factor: The Science of Creating High-Performance Companies*. Amacom.

CHAPTER III: Has Money Toppled *Eudaimonia*?

16. Romano, L. (2010). *Proceedings of the 6th International Congress of the Archaeology of the Ancient Near East*, vol. 3. Otto Harrassowitz Verlag.

17. Ben-Shahar, T.; *loc. cit.* p. 40.

18. Easterlin, R. A and Sawangfa, O. (2010): "Happiness and Economic Growth: ¿Does the Cross Section Predict Time Trends? Evidence from Developing Countries", en Diener, E., Heliwell, J. F and Kahneman, D. (eds.), *International Differences in Well-being. Oxford University Press*. Retrieved from https://doi.org/10.1093/acprof:oso/9780199732739.003.0007.

19. Capponi, R. (2019). *Felicidad Sólida: sobre la construcción de una felicidad perdurable*. Zig Zag.

20. Retrieved from https://www.ted.com/talks/dan_gilbert_the_surprising_science_of_fulfillment?

21. Ben-Shahar, T.; *loc. cit.* p. 40.

22. Capponi, R; *loc. cit.* p. 49.

23. Diener, E. and Seligman, M. E. P. (2004). "Beyond Money: Toward an Economy of Well-Being". *Psychological Science in the*

Public Interest 5(1), p. 1-31. Retrieved from https://doi.org/10.1111/j.0963-7214.2004.00501001.x

24. Brickman, P., Coates, D. y Janoff-Bulman, R. (1978). "Lottery Winners and Accident Victims: Is Happiness relative?". *Journal of Personality and Social Psychology 36*(8), p. 917-927. https://doi.org/10.1037/0022-3514.36.8.917.

25. Retrieved from https://www.annualreviews.org/doi/pdf/10.1146/annurev-psych-122414-033344.

26. Kasser, T., Ryan, R. M., Couchman, C. E. and Sheldon, K. M. (2004). "Materialistic Values: Their Causes and Consequences", in T. Kasser y A. D. Kanner (eds.). *Psychology and Consumer Culture: The Struggle for a Good Life in a Materialistic World*. American Psychological Association. https://doi.org/10.1037/10658-002.

27. Ben-Shahar, T.; *loc. cit.* p. 40.

28. Tolle E. (2005). *A New Earth: Awakening to Your Life's Purpose.* Namaste Publishing.

29. Caprariello, P. A. and Reis, H. T. (2013). "To Do, to Have, or to Share? Valuing Experiences Over Material Possessions Depends on the Involvement of Others". *Journal of Personality and Social Psychology* 104(2), p. 199-215. / Dunn, E. W., Aknin, L. B. and Norton, M. I. (2008). "Spending Money on Others Promotes Happiness". Science 319, p. 1687–1688.

30. Philanthropic campaign started in June 2010 by American billionaires Warren Buffett and Bill Gates. The official website begins by stating that it is "a commitment by the world's wealthiest individuals and families to dedicate the majority of their wealth to giving back." www.givingpledge.org.

CHAPTER IV: Existential Vacuum

31. Viktor Frankl is, to many, the father of purpose. He was the first to create a theory around this concept in the modern Western world, which led him to develop his own psychological trend based on the meaning or purpose of life, associating it to a specific kind of therapy: logotherapy. It starts from the premise that men not only

seek pleasure (Freud's postulate) or power (Adler's hypothesis) but also, and above all, to attach meaning to life.

32. Frankl, V. (2006). Man's Search for Meaning. Beacon Press.

33. Andresen, J. J. (1999). *"Awe and the Transforming of Awarenesses"*. Contemporary Psychoanalysis 35, pag. 507-521. / Freud S. (1926) A Romain Rolland. O.C. de Sigmund Freud. Biblioteca Nueva.

34. This feeling of unity with all that which exists has been given different names: universal intelligence, collective consciousness, planetary consciousness, spirit, God, one, all, superior purpose.

35. Fromm, E. (2006). The Art of Loving. Harper Perennial Modern Classics.

36. Bronk, K. C. (2011). The Role of Purpose in Life in Healthy Identity Formation: A Grounded Model. New Directions for Youth Development 132, pag. 31–44. https://doi.org/10.1002/yd.426 / Burrow, A. L. y Hill, P. L. (2011). "Purpose as a Form of Identity Capital for Positive Youth Adjustment". Developmental Psychology, 47(4), pag. 1196-1206. https://doi.org/10.1037/a0023818. / Hill, P. L., Sumner, R. Y Burrow, A. L. (2014) "Understanding the Pathways to Purpose: Examining Personality and Well-being Correlates Across Adulthood". The Journal of Positive Psychology 9:3, pag. 227-234. / Damon, W. (2008). *The Path to Purpose: Helping Our Children Find Their Calling in Life*. Free Press / Bloom, B. S. (1985). *Developing in Talent in Young People*. Ballantine Books.

37. Arnett, J. J. (2000). *Optimistic Bias in Adolescent and Adult Smokers and Nonsmokers*. Addictive Behaviors 25(4), pag. 625–632. https://doi.org/10.1016/s0306-4603(99)00072-6.

38. Bronk, K. C. (2011). *A Grounded Theory of the Development of Noble Youth Purpose*. Journal of Adolescent Research 27(1), pag. 78–109.

39. Erikson, E. H. (1968). *Identity: Youth and Crisis*. W.W. Norton.

40. Baumeister, R. (1992). *Meaning in Life*. The Guilford Press.

41. Fromm, E.; *loc. cit.* p. 61.

42. Frankl, V. E. (1979). *The Unheard Cry for Meaning: Psychotherapy and Humanism*. Touchstone.

43. Bronk, K. C. (2014). Purpose in Life. Springer. / Bronk, K. C. (2013). *Purpose in Life: A Critical Component of Optimal Youth Development*. Springer Science & Business Media. pag. 55.

44. Bronk, K. C. et al. (2010). *"The Prevalence of a Purpose in Life Among High Ability Adolescents"*. High Ability Studies 21 (2), pag. 133-145. / Damon, W. The Path to Purpose. Free Press/ Francis L. J. (2000). *"The Relationship Between Bible Reading and Purpose in Life Among 13- to-15- Years Old"*. Mental Health, Religion, and Culture 3, pag. 27-36. / Moran, S. (2009).

45. 2019 Workforce Purpose Index - Pathways to Fulfillment at Work. Retrieved from https://www.imperative.com. Founded in 2014, Imperative is a platform for the transformation of organizational culture, which places purpose at the center of its strategy, and which has carried out various studies on the subject.

46. Most of the studies on the subject have focused on promoting significant experiences in young people, since it has been shown that experiences of this type (volunteering, religious education, community life, housework, etc.) promote a healthy formation of identity that facilitates the transition to adulthood and which depends largely on the environment in which young people develop this sense of purpose.

47. Bronson, P. (2002). *What Should I Do with My Life?* Random House.

CHAPTER V: Starting A Path

48. Kashdan, T. B. y McKnight, P. E. (2009). *"Origins of Purpose in Life: Refining Our Understanding of a Life Well Lived"*. Psychological Topics 18, pag. 303-316. / Steger, M. F., Kashdan, T. B., Sullivan, B. A. y Lorentz, D. (2008). *"Understanding the Search for Meaning in Life: Personality, Cognitive Style, and the Dynamic Between Seeking and Experiencing Meaning"*. Journal of Personality 76(2), pag. 199-228. / Kashdan, T. B. y Steger, M. F. (2007). *"Curiosity and Pathways to Bell-being and Meaning in Life: Traits, States, and Everyday Behaviors"*. Motivation and Emotion 31, pag. 159-173.

49. May, P. (2019). *De la tierra al alma: el camino humano al despertar de la conciencia espiritual*. Urano.

50. The Comunidad Organizaciones Solidarias [Community of Solidary Organizations], better known as "COS," is a space for meeting, collaborating and articulating civil society organizations that work at the service of people in situations of poverty and / or social exclusion in Chile. It is constituted by over two hundred organizations which bring together more than eleven thousand workers and seventeen thousand volunteers who, together, collaborate with more than nine hundred thousand users. Its website is http://comunidad-org.cl/.

51. Fundación Nuestros Hijos [Our Children Foundation]: http://www.fnh.cl/.

52. Oprah Winfrey, born in 1954, is an American journalist, television presenter, producer, actress, businesswoman, philanthropist and book critic. She was won multiple Emmy Awards for her show *The Oprah Winfrey Show*, the most watched in television history. She is also recognized as the richest African American woman and the most influential communicator in the United States.

53. It is the root of the word teleology, a term that means the study or doctrine of intentionality, or the study of objects based on their objectives, purposes or intentions. Teleology is a central concept for Aristotle in biology and in his theory of causation.

CHAPTER VI: The Path To Purpose

54. Fromm, E.; *loc. cit p.* 61.

55. Baumeister, R. F.; *loc. cit p.* 37.

56. Sokolowski, R. (2013). *Phenomenology of the Human Person.* Cambridge University Press.

57. Our intention isn't the same as our wishes, notwithstanding that they may coincide many times. Desires are rather impulses that seek to get us closer to pleasure and away from pain, and that can be about impossible things that depend on circumstances or others; unlike intention, which is based on what is good and achievable by ourselves. Aristotle, *Nicomachean Ethics*. Third book, chapter V.

58. Hofmann, W. y Wilson, T. D. (2010). *"Consciousness, Introspection, and the Adaptive Unconsciousness."* En B. Gawronski y B. K. Payne (eds.). *Handbook of Implicit Social Cognition:*

Measurement, Theory, and Applications. Guilford Press. / Kahneman, D. (2011). *Thinking, Fast and Slow.* Farrar, Straus and Giroux.

59. Wilson, T. D. y Gilbert, D. T. (2005). *"Affective Forecasting: Knowing What to Want".* Current Directions in Psychological Science 14, pag. 131-134.

60. Ryan, R. M., Sheldon, K. M., Kasser, T. y Deci, E. L. (1996). *"All Goals are Not Created Equal: The Relation of Goal Content and Regulatory Styles to Mental Health".* En Bargh, J. A. y Gollwitzer, P. M. (eds.). *The Psychology of Action: Linking Cognition and Motivation to Behavior.* Guilford Press.

61. George, L. K. (2000). *"Well-being and Sense of Self: What We Know, What We Need to Know".* En Schaie, K.W. y Hendricks, J. (eds.). *The Evolution of the Aging Self.* Springer.

62. When Aristotle discusses friendship, he refers to all sorts of relationships based on a non-romantic love.

63. Grant. A (abril 2013). *"In the Company of Givers and Takers".* Harvard Busssines Review 91(4):90-7, pag. 142.

64. Zak, P. (2017). *Trust Factor: The Science of Creating High-Performance Companies.* Amacom.

65. Vallacher, R. R. y Wegner, D. M. (1987). *"What do People Think They're Doing? Action Identification and Human Behavior".* Psychological Review 94(1), pag. 3–15. https://doi.org/10.1037/0033-295x.94.1.3.

66. Wrzesniewski, A., McCauley, C., Rozin, P. y Schwartz, B. (1997). *"Jobs, Careers, and Callings: People's Relations to Their Work".* Journal of Research in Personality 31(1), pag. 21–33. https://doi.org/10.1006/jrpe.1997.2162.

67. Manson, M. (2016). *The Subtle Art of Not Giving a F*ck: A Counterintuitive Approach to Living a Good Life.* Harper.

CHAPTER VII: Who Am I? Authenticity And Passion

68. Hernández de la Fuente, D. (2008). *Oráculos griegos.* Alianza. / Plutarco (1995). *Obras morales y de costumbres VI.* Gredos.

69. Carver, C. S. y Scheier, M. F. (2002). *"Optimism"*. En Snyder, C. R. y López, S. J. (eds.). *Handbook of Positive Psychology*. Oxford University Press.

70. Tolle, E..; *loc. cit.* p. 53.

71. Chopra, D (2012). *Spiritual Solutions*. Harmony Books.

72 . Tolle, E.; *loc. cit.* p. 53.

73. Enric Corbera Institute, Corbera, E., Corbera, D., Batlló, M., Villalobos, V., Aguilar, C.,y Nuñez, P. (2017). *Bioneuroemoción: Un método para el bienestar emocional.* Ediciones El Grano de Mostaza.

74. Nussbaum, M. C. (2009). *The Therapy of Desire: Theory and Practice in Hellenistic Ethics.* Princeton University Press.

75. Marías, J. (1993). *Mapa del mundo personal.* Alianza.

76. Ware, B. (2019). *Top Five Regrets of the Dying: A Life Transformed by the Dearly Departing.* Hay House Inc.

77. Personal interview conducted with Ely Rudnick, on May 20th, 2020.

78. https://www.burntogive.com/about. By June 1st, 2020.

79. We will talk about the fourth element, contributing to the world, when we deal with transcendence.

80. Vallerand, R. J., et al. (2203). *"Les passions de Láme: On obsessive and harmonious passion"*. Journal of Personality and Social Psychology, 85 (4), pag. 756-767.

81. Andreatta, B. (2018). *Wired to Connect: The Brain Science of Teams and a New Model for Creating Collaboration and Inclusion.* 7th Mind Publishing; Study PwC. Making Work More Meaningful: Building a Fulfilling Employee Experience. https://www.pwc.com/us/en/library/workforce-of-the-future/fulfillment-at-work.html.

82. Bronk, K. C.; *loc. cit.* p. 63.

83. Bronk, K. C. (2011). *A Grounded Theory of the Development of Noble Youth Purpose.* Journal of Adolescent Research, 27(1), pag.

78–109. / Damon, W. (2008). *The Path to Purpose: Helping Our Children Find Their Calling in Life*. Free Press.

84. Grant, A. (2014). *Give and Take: Why Helping Others Drives Our Success*. Penguin Books.

85. Fromm, E.; *loc. cit.* p. 61.

86. Niemiec, R. M., y McGrath, R. E. (2019). *The Power of Character Strengths: Appreciate and Ignite Your Positive Personality*. VIA Institute on Character.

87. Clifton, D. O., Anderson, E. C. y Schreiner, L. A. (2016). *Strengths Quest: Discover and Develop Your Strengths in Academics, Career, and Beyond*. Gallup Press.

88. Clifton, D. O., Anderson, E. C. y Schreiner, L. A.; *loc. cit.* p. 131.

89. Csíkszentmihályi, M. (2008). *Flow: The Psychology of Optimal Experience*. Harper Perennial Modern Classics.

90. Term coined by my dear friend Pablo Sepúlveda.

91. Duckworth, A. (2018). *Grit: The Power of Passion and Perseverance*. Scribner.

92. www.interpreta.org.

93. Tips by Ely Rudnick from our personal interview on May 20th 2020.

CHAPTER VIII: My Place In The World. Meaning Of Life And Transcendence

94. Reker, G. T. y Peacock, E. J. (1981). *The Life Attitude Profile (LAP): A Multidimensional Instrument for Assessing Attitudes Toward Life*. Canadian Journal of Behavioural Science/Revue Canadienne Des Sciences Du Comportement 13(3), pag. 264–273.

95. Heintzelman, S. J. y King, L. A. (2014). *"(The Feeling of) Meaning-as-Information"*. Personality and Social Psychology Review 18(2), pag. 153-67. / Hicks, J. A., Cicero, D. C., Trent, J., Burton, C. M. y King, L. A. (2010). *"Positive Affect, Intuition, and the Feeling*

of Meaning". Journal of Personality and Social Psychology 98, pag. 967-979.

96. Steger, M. F., Frazier, P., Oishi, S., y Kaler, M. (2006). *"The Meaning in Life Questionnaire: Assessing the Presence of and Search for Meaning in Life"*. Journal of Counseling Psychology 53, pag. 80–93.

97. Steger, M.F. (2012). *"Experiencing Meaning in Life: Optimal Functioning at the Nexus of Spirituality, Psychopathology, and Wellbeing"*, en Wong, P. T. P. y Fry, P. S. (eds.). *The human Quest for Meaning*. Routledge.

98. Csíkszentmihályi, M. *loc. cit.* p. 134.

99. Harari, Y. N. (2019). *21 Lessons for the 21st Century*. Random House.

100. Steger, M. F., Frazier, P., Oishi, S. y Kaler, M.; *loc. cit.* p. 146.

101. Antonovsky, A. (1991). *"The Structural Resources of Salutogenic Strengths"*, en Cooper, C. L. y Payne, R. (eds.). *Personality and Stress: Individual Differences in the Stress Process*. L. Wiley.

102. Stefanetti, C. "El Ángel del gueto de Varsovia' candidata al Nobel de la Paz". http://www.elaguilablanca.com/glospolski/ glospolski-nota0011.html.

103. We'll use Maslow's pyramid. The most basic needs, those related to survival, aren't considered a source of meaning, because we're already biologically predisposed for them, which is why we don't need to make sense out of them in order to want to satisfy them. We seek for sustenance merely because it's fundamental for our survival. Neuroscience has managed to prove the way certain chemical substances, like dopamine and endorphins, regard us when we lean towards those behaviors that are essential for our survival. See Table N°1 for more details on different author's opinions on the different sources of meaning.

104. Andreatta, B. (2018). *Wired to connect: The Brain Science of Teams*. 7th Mind Publishing.

105. Manson, M. *op cit* p. 92.

106. Madanes, C. (2009). *Relationship Breakthrough: How to create outstanding relationship in every area of your life.* Rodale.

107. Madanes, C.; *loc. cit.* p. 151.

108. Wong, P. T. P., Wong, L. C. J. y McDonald, M. J. (2012). *The Positive Psychology of Meaning and Spirituality: Selected Papers from Meaning Conferences.* Purpose Research.

109. Frankl, V. E. (2014). *The Will to Meaning: Foundations and Applications of Logotherapy.* Plume.

110. He also realized that while some of them didn't transcend their own interests, they lived a quiet life, making good use of their capabilities. He called this group "healthy people." James, W. (1902). *The Varieties of Religious Experience.* Harvard University Press.

111. Maslow, A. H. (1994). *Religions, Values, and Peak-Experiences (Compass).* Penguin Books.

112. Maslow, A. H., Maslow, B. G. y Geiger, H. (1993). *The Farther Reaches of Human Nature.* Penguin / Arkana.

113. Bronk, K. C., Holmes Finch, W. y Talib, T. L. (2010). *"Purpose in Life Among High Ability Adolescents"*. High Ability Studies 21(2), pag. 133–145. https://doi.org/10.1080/13598139.2010.525339. / Mariano, J. M. y Vaillant, G. E. (2012). *"Youth Purpose Among the 'Greatest Generation'"*. The Journal of Positive Psychology 7(4), pag. 281–293. https://doi.org/10.1080/17439760.2012.686624. / Duckworth, A.; *loc. cit.* p. 136.

114. Madanes, C., y Robbins, A. (2009). *Relationship Breakthrough: How to Create Outstanding Relationship in Every Area of Your Life.* Rodale Books.

115. McCullough, M. E. y Snyder, C. R. (2000). *"Classical Source of Human Strength: Revisiting an Old Home and Building a New One"*. Journal of Social and Clinical Psychology 19(1), pag. 1–10. https://doi.org/10.1521/jscp.2000.19.1.1.

116. https://brenebrown.com/definitions/.

117. Feather, N. T. (1992). *"Values, Valences, Expectations, and Actions"*. Journal of Social Issues 48, pag. 109-124.

118. Shalom Schwartz has derived ten generic, basic and universal values from the human condition, but adds that it is highly likely that the weight given to each of them differs from culture to culture. Schwartz, S. H. (1992). "Universals in the Content and Structure of Values: Theory and Empirical Tests in 20 Countries", en M. Zanna (ed.). *Advances in Experimental Social Psychology* (Vol. 25). Academic Press.

119. Damon, W.; *loc. cit.* p. 64. / Damon, W. (2003). *Noble Purpose: Joy of Living a Meaningful Life*. Templeton Foundation Press. / Damon, W., Menon, J. and Bronk, K. C. (2003). "The Development of Purpose During Adolescence". Applied Developmental Science. doi:10.1207/S1532480XADS0703_2.

120. They based their selection on the criteria established by Anne Colby and William Damon. Colby, A., and Damon, W. (1994). *Some Do Care: Contemporary Lives of Moral Commitment*. Free Press.

121. Frimer, J A., Walker, L. J., Dunlop, W. L., Lee, B. H. y Riches, A. (2011). *"The Integration of Agency and Communion in Moral Personality: Evidence of Enlightened Self-interest"*. Journal of Personality and Social Psychology 101 (1), pag. 149-163.

122. Hood, R. W., Jr., Hill, P. C. y Spilka, B. (2009). *Psychology of Religion: An Empirical Approach*. Guilford Press.

123. This chart has been adapted from Yaden et al. (2017) by Scott Barry Kaufman for his book *Transcend*. It has likewise been adapted for this book. It suggests a scale of transcendental experiences with levels of connection to the world.

124. Kaufman, S. B. (2020). *Transcend: The New Science of Self-Actualization*. Tarcher Perigee. / Yaden, D. B., Haidt, J., Hood, R. W., Vago, D. R. y Newberg, A. B. (1° de mayo de 2017). *"The Varieties of Self-Transcendent Experience"*. Review of General Psychology. Advance online publication. http://dx.doi.org/10.1037/gpr0000102.

125. These transcendent experiences are comprised of two elements: a) an annihilatory one, which refers both to the dissolution of the bodily sense of self, accompanied by the reduction of its limits and self-sufficiency; and b) a relational component, which refers to the sense of connection, even to the point of fusion, with something beyond the self, generally other people and aspects of one's environment. Both components can occur in varying degrees and, although it remains an

open question for investigation, these aspects can vary correlatively or independently of each other.

126. Kaufman, S. B., *loc. cit.* p. 176.

127. Miller, W. R. y C'de Baca, J. (2001). *Quantum Change: When Epiphanies and Sudden Insights Transform Ordinary Lives*. Guilford Press.

128. www.inmi.cl

129. Grant, A.; *loc. cit.* p. 128.

130. *Two Great Forces of Human Nature: Bill Gates, "Creative Capitalism,"* World Economic Forum, 24 de enero de 2008.

131. Bakan, D. (1966). *The Duality of Human Existence: Isolation and Communion in Western Man*. Bacon Press.

132. Kaufman, B. S.; *loc. cit.* p. 176.

CHAPTER X: Motivation, The Best Sign That You're On Your Way

133. Deci, E. L. y Ryan, R.M. (1985). *Intrinsic Motivation and Self-Determination in Human Behavior. Perspectives in Social Psychology.* Springer.

134. Optimal challenges understood as the highest level of functioning, especially in our relationships, work, education and feeling of well-being. https://dictionary.apa.org/optimal-functioning.

135. Deci, E. L. y Ryan, R. M. (2000). *"The `What´ and `Why´ of Goal Pursuits: Human Needs and the Self-Determination of Behavior"*. Psychological Inquiry 11, pag. 227-268. / Sheldon, K. M. (2004). Optimal Human Being: An Integrated Multilevel Perspective. Lawrence Erlbaum. / Sheldon, K. M. (2011). *"Integrating Behavioral-motive and Experiential-requirement Perspectives on Psychological Needs: A two Process Perspective"*. Psychological Review 118, pag. 552-569. / Gardner, H. (2006). Multiple Intelligences: New Horizons in Theory and Practice. Basic Books. / Duckworth, A.; *loc. cit.* p. 136 / Vallerand, R. J., et al. (2203). *"Les passions de Láme: On obsessive and harmonious passion"*. Journal of Personality and Social Psychology 85

(4), pag. 756-767. / Sheldon, K. M. y Kasser, T. (1995). *"Coherence and Congruence: Two Aspects of Personality Integration"*. Journal of Personality and Social Psychology 68, pag. 531-543.

136. Ambrose, M. L. y Kulik, C. T. (1999). *"Old Friends, New Faces: Motivation Research in the 1990´s"*. Journal of Management 25(3), p. 231–292. https://doi.org/10.1177/014920639902500302.

137. Amabile, T. M. (1997). *"Motivating Creativity in Organizations: On Doing What You Love and Loving What You Do"*. California Management Review 40(1), pag. 39–58. https://doi.org/10.2307/41165921.

138. Tolle, E.; *loc. cit.* p. 53.

139. Crumbaugh, J. C. (1977). *"The Seeking of Noetic Goals Test (SONG): A Complementary Scale to Purpose in Life Test (PIL)"*. Journal of Clinical Psychology 33, pag. 900-907. http://dx.doi.org/10.1002/1097-4679(197707)33:3<900::AID-JCLP2270330362>3.0.CO;2-8.

140. Capponi, R.; *loc. cit.* p. 49.

141. Sheldon, K. M.; *loc. cit.* p. 154. / Sheldon, K. M. (2009). *"Goal-striving Across the Life-span: Do People Learn to Select More Self-concordant Goals as They Age?"*, en M. C., Smith y T. G., Reio (eds.). The Handbook of Research on Adult Development and Learning. Routledge. / Sheldon, K. M. y Elliot, A. J. (1999). *"Goal Striving, Need-satisfaction, and Longitudinal Well-being: The Self-concordance Model"*. Journal of Personality and Social Psychology 76, pag. 482-497.

142. Sheldon, K. M. (2014). *"Becoming Oneself"*. Personality and Social Psychology Review 18(4), pag. 349–365. https://doi.org/10.1177/1088868314538549. / Epstein, S. (2014). *Cognitive-experiential Theory: An Integrative Theory of Personality*. Oxford University Press. www.viacharacter.org/research/findings.

143. Kahneman, D. y Fredrick, S. (2005). *"A Model of Heuristic Judgment"*, en Holyoak, K. J. y Morrison, R. G. (eds.). The Cambridge Handbook of Thinking and Reasoning. Cambridge University Press. / Stanovich, K. E. y West, R. F. (2000). *"Individual Difference in Reasoning: Implications for the Rationality Debate?"*. Behavioral & Brain Sciences 23, pag. 645-726.

144. Gawronski, B. y Bodenhausen, G. V. (2012). *"Self-insight From a Dual-process Perspective"*, en Vazire, S. y Wilson, T. D. (eds.). *Handbook of Self-knowledge* (pag. 22-38). Guilford Press.

145. One of the explanations for the unconscious lies in the idea that the cognitive brain controls the ability to temper our emotional reactions. This capacity, on the one hand, is positive, since it avoids relational problems by allowing us to regulate and control our impulses. However, when we repress them, they pass into the unconscious and are waiting to emerge at a more convenient time. If this occasion doesn't come, an internal inconsistency is generated. This, in turn, causes sustained stress over time, which generates other types of problems. Institute, Enric Corbera, Corbera, E., Corbera, D., Batlló, M., Villalobos, V., Aguilar, C. and Nuñez, P. (2017). *Bioneuroemoción: Un método para el bienestar emocional*. Ediciones El Grano de Mostaza.

146. Sheldon, K. M.; *loc. cit.* p. 159.

147. Sheldon, K. M. y Elliot, A. J. (1998). *"Not All Personal Goals are Personal: Comparing Autonomous and Controlled Reasons as Predictors of Effort and Attainment"*. Personality and Social Psychology Bulletin 24, pag. 546-557. / Sheldon, K. M. y Kasser, T. (1998). *"Pursuing Personal Goals: Skills Enable Progress, But Not All Progress is Beneficial"*. Personality and Social Psychology Bulletin 24, pag. 1319-1331.

148. Burton, C. M. (2008). *"Gut Feelings and Goal Pursuit: A Path to Selfconcordance"*. Dissertation Abstracts International: Section B. Sciences and Engineering 73(2-B), pag. 1303-1387.

149. Sheldon, K. M. y Krieger, L. (2004). *"Does Law School Undermine Law Students? Examining Changes in Goals, Values, and Wellbeing"*. Behavioral Sciences & the Law 22, pag. 261-286.

150. Parker, S. K., Bindl, U. K. y Strauss, K. (2010). *"Making Things Happen: A Model of Proactive Motivation"*. Journal of Management 36, p. 827-856. / Greguras, G. J. y Diefendorff, J. M. (2010). *"Why Does Proactive Personality redict Employee Life Satisfaction and Work Behaviors? A Field Investigation of the Mediating Role of the Selfconcordance Model"*. Personnel Psychology 63, pag. 539-560. / Bateman, T. S. y Crant, J. M. (1993). *"The Proactive Component of Organizational Behavior: A Measure and Correlates"*. Journal of Organizational Behavior 14, pag. 103-118.

151. Judge, J. A., Bono, J. E., Erez, A. y Locke, E. A. (2005). *"Core Self-evaluations and Job and Life Satisfaction: The Role of Selfconcordance and Goal Attainment"*. Journal of Applied Psychology 90, pag. 257-268.

CHAPTER XI: Spoiler Alert! Purpose Wasn't What I Thought It Would Be, But I Discovered So Much More

152. Suma teológica, I-II, q. 26 art.4.

153. Quatre-vingt-un-chapitres sur l'esprit et les passions, V, 4, *Bibl. de la Pléiade, Les passions et la sagesse*, pág. 1199.

154. Based on the books by Miguel Ruiz: *Los cuatro acuerdos y La maestría del amor.* Editorial Amber-Allen Publishing.

155. Fromm, E.; *loc. cit.* p. 61.

156. Comte-Sponville, A.; Corral, C. B. y Corral, C. M. (2014b). *Pequeño tratado de las grandes virtudes.* Paidós.

157. Kant, I. (1797). Doctrina de la virtud, introducción, XII, c.

158. Fromm, E.; *loc. cit.* p. 61.

159. Sartre, J. P. (1905-1980). *El ser y la nada. Ensayo de ontología fenomenológica.* Editorial Losada.

160. Chopra, D. (1994). *The Seven Spiritual Laws of Success: A Practical Guide to the Fulfillment of Your Dreams.* New World Library / Amber-Allen Publishing.

161. Manson, M.; *loc. cit.* p. 92.

162. The book *Have You Filled Your Bucket Today*, by author Carol McCloud, was first published in 2006 to teach young girls and boys how, when you worry about others and show them your love in the things you say and do, you are happier. Since then, it has spread around the world to help millions of people of all ages to live more fulfilling lives. The bucket, which is invisible to the eye, represents mental and emotional health.

APPENDIX I: Ikigai And The Golden Circle

163. García, H. y Miralles, F. (2017). *Ikigai: The Japanese Secret to a Long and Happy Life*. Penguin.

164. The study also includes the island of Sardinia (Italy), Loma Linda (California, United States), Nicoya (Costa Rica) and the island of Icaria (Greece). Buettner, D. (2005, November). "Longevity, The Secrets of Long Life." National Geographic Magazine.

165. This concept is very important when it comes to differentiating our Purpose from our hobbies and volunteering.

166. The available literature doesn't offer an analysis of the combination between 1) what you're good at and what the world needs; and 2) what you love and what you can get paid for.

167. A very similar scheme called The Hedgehog was developed by Jim Collins in his book Good to Great (2009). It consists of three elements: what you are passionate about, what you are the best in the world at, and what motivates you financially.

168. This last conclusion is the author's, and not part of *ikigai's* philosophy.

169. Sinek, S. (2011). *Start with Why: How Great Leaders Inspire Everyone to Take Action*. Portfolio. / Sinek, S. (2017). *Leaders Eat Last: Why Some Teams Pull Together and Others Don't*. Portfolio.

APPENDIX II: Definitions Of Purpose

170. *Journal of Personality and Social Psychology 57*(6), pag. 1069-1081.

171. *Psychological Topics 18*(2), George Mason University, pag. 303-316.

172. *Journal of Management, Spirituality & Religion 8*(4), pag. 281-297.

APPENDIX III: Abraham Maslow's Theory Z

173. *Psychiatry 36*(4), pag. 409–427. https://doi.org/10.1080/00332 747.1973.11023774.

174. *Journal of Gerontology* 42(1), pag. 44-49. https://doi.org/10.1093/geronj/42.1.44.

175. *Journal of Clinical Psychology* 20(2), pag. 200-207.

176. *The Journal of Positive Psychology* 8(5), pag. 365–375.

177. Maslow, A. H.; *loc. cit.* p. 168.

APPENDIX IV: Levels Of Transcendence

178. Davidson, R. J., Kabat-Zinn, J., Schumacher, J., Rosenkranz, M., Muller, D., Santorelli, S. F., . . . Sheridan, J. F. (2003). *"Alterations in Brain and Immune Function Produced by Mindfulness Meditation"*. Psychosomatic Medicine 65, p. 564–570. http://dx.doi.org/10.1097/01.PSY.0000077505.67574.E3. / Jha, A. P., Krompinger, J. y Baime, M. J. (2007). *"Mindfulness Training Modifies Subsystems of Attention"*. Cognitive, Affective & Behavioral Neuroscience 7, pag. 109–119. http://dx.doi.org/10.3758/CABN.7.2.109. / Kabat-Zinn, J. (1994). *Wherever You Go, There You Are: Mindfulness Meditation in Everyday Life*. Hyperion.

179. Emmons, R. (2008). *Thanks!: How Practicing Gratitude Can Make You Happier.* Mariner Books.

180. Rudd, M., Vohs, K. D. y Aaker, J. (2012). *"Awe Expands People's Perception of Time, Alters Decision Making, and Enhances Well-being"*. Psychological Science 23, pag. 1130 –1136. http://dx.doi.org/10.1177/ 0956797612438731.

181. Keltner, D. y Haidt, J. (2003). *"Approaching Awe, a Moral, Spiritual, and Aesthetic Emotion"*. Cognition and Emotion 17, pag. 297–314. http://dx.doi.org/10.1080/026999930302297.

182. Yaden, D. B., Iwry, J., Slack, K. J., Eichstaedt, J. C., Zhao, Y., Vaillant, G. E. y Newberg, A. B. (2016a). *"The Overview Effect: Awe and Self-transcendent Experience in Space Flight"*. Psychology of Consciousness: Theory, Research, and Practice 3, pag. 1–11. http://dx.doi.org/10.1037/cns0000086.

183. Belzak, W. C. M., Thrash, T. M., Sim, Y. Y. y Wadsworth, L. M. (2017). *"Beyond Hedonic and Eudaimonic Well-Being: Inspiration and the Self-Transcendence Tradition"*. The Happy Mind:

Cognitive Contributions to Well-Being, pag. 117–138. https://doi.org/10.1007/978-3-319-58763-9_7.

184. Thrash, T. M. y Elliot, A. J. (2003). *"Inspiration as a Psychological Construct"*. Journal of Personality and Social Psychology 84(4), pag. 871–889. https://doi.org/10.1037/0022-3514.84.4.871.

185. Buechner, F. (1973). *Wishful Thinking: A Theological ABC*. Harper.

186. Erikson, E. y Erikson, J. (1981). *"On Generativity and Identity: From a Conversation with Erik and Joan Erikson"*. Harvard Educational Review 51(2), pag. 249–269. https://doi.org/10.17763/haer.51.2.g211757u27732p67.

TABLE 1

187. Maslow, A. H.; *loc. cit.* p. 168.

188. Kaufman, S.B.; *loc. cit.* p. 147.

189. Keyes, C. L. M. y Haidt, J. (eds.). *Flourishing: Positive Psychology and the Life Well-lived*. American Psychological Association, pag. 105–128. https://doi.org/10.1037/10594-005.

190. Klinger, E. (1998). *The Human Quest for Meaning: A Handbook of Psychological Research and Clinical Applications*, Lawrence Erlbaum Associates Publishers. p. 27–50.

191. *Psychological Reports* 49(1), p. 87–90. https://doi.org/10.2466/pr0.1981.49.1.87.

192. Bronk, K. C.; *loc. cit.* p. 48. p. 63.

193. Psychological inquiry 9(1), p. 1-28.

194. Educational Gerontology 30(9), p. 751–766.

A Crane Among Chickens

A Living Record of Friendship Shared Across Cultures

Carolyn Oliver